Alliances, Coalitions
and Partnerships

Alliances, Coalitions *and* Partnerships

BUILDING COLLABORATIVE ORGANIZATIONS

Joan M. Roberts

NEW SOCIETY PUBLISHERS

Cataloguing in Publication Data:
A catalog record for this publication is available from the National Library of
Canada.

Cover design by Diane McIntosh. Cover Image: Digital Vision.

Printed in Canada by Friesens Inc.

New Society Publishers acknowledges the support of the Government of
Canada through the Book Publishing Industry Development Program (BPIDP)
for our publishing activities.

Paperback ISBN: 0-86571-516-5

Inquiries regarding requests to reprint all or part of *Alliances, Coalitions* and
Partnerships should be addressed to New Society Publishers at the address below.

To order directly from the publishers, please add $4.50 shipping to the price of
the first copy, and $1.00 for each additional copy (plus GST in Canada). Send
check or money order to:

New Society Publishers
P.O. Box 189, Gabriola Island, BC V0R 1X0, Canada
1-800-567-6772

New Society Publishers' mission is to publish books that contribute in fundamental ways to building an ecologically sustainable and just society, and to do so
with the least possible impact on the environment, in a manner that models this
vision. We are committed to doing this not just through education, but through
action. We are acting on our commitment to the world's remaining ancient forests
by phasing out our paper supply from ancient forests worldwide. This book is one
step towards ending global deforestation and climate change. It is printed on acid-
free paper that is **100% old growth forest-free** (100% post-consumer recycled),
processed chlorine free, and printed with vegetable based, low VOC inks. For further information, or to browse our full list of books and purchase securely, visit
our website at: www.newsociety.com
NEW SOCIETY PUBLISHERS   www.newsociety.com

To the memory of the former City of York,
and all who lived and worked there!

Contents

Acknowledgments

This book is the result of two years of fascinating work. In it, I share learning from over 20 years in community development and large system change. This learning and experience is the result of all those who partnered, hired, voted or supported me in all my endeavors. Thank you for believing in me.

Thanks, too, to Chris Plant at New Society Publishers for believing I could produce this book. I want also to thank my editors at New Society, Audrey McLellan and Ingrid Witvoet for their owl-like eyes.

Thanks go to Patrick Cavalier for reviewing the manuscript, providing a sounding board and valuable feedback on my interdisplinary concepts and Dorothy Aaron for early editing and advice.

Gratitude is also extended to to all my workshop participants that field tested the concepts in this book and posed difficult questions.

Lastly, I want to thank my children Erin and Neil Mentuch, for being wonderful young adults, for their ongoing support and for giving me the space to assume the various roles and opportunities my life has presented.

Introduction

Nothing in the world can take the place of persistence...
Talent will not, nothing is more common than unsuccessful men with talent.
Genius will not; unrewarded genius is almost a proverb.
Education will not. The world is full of educated derelicts.
Persistence and determination alone are omnipotent. The slogan "press on" has
solved, and always will solve, the problems of the human race

Calvin Coolidge

This is a book about an emerging form of organization — an organization of organizations or a group of groups that come together to collaborate. There is not yet a consensus on nomenclature for these new organizations. They are sometimes called *coalitions* when they are developed to achieve health or public policy outcomes. They may be called *alliances* when organized to operate joint programming initiatives. The catchall terms *network* and *partnership* are also used when two or more organizations come together to operate for mutual benefit. All of these forms of organization originate from other organizations and have accountabilities and feedback loops to their organizations of origin.

Organizations of organizations have always existed. In political terms, they are called *federations*. King Arthur's Round Table (of knights) was an organization of local tribal and political leaders who came together for common objectives, in their case to protect their territories. Most modern nation-states evolved from the merging of existing organizations — local tribes or ethnic groups organized into a higher-level political body. What is new is that we are now developing this form of organization at the grassroots level of business and non-profit service delivery.

I have been involved in developing this type of organization for many years, yet I never had much guidance on how to do it. *Why* I needed to do it seemed obvious any time I sat at a table with others intent on solving a complex social problem. None of us had enough resources or know-how to go it alone. Inter-organizational collaboration seemed the practical and right thing to do, and so we did it.

I have worked often and successfully with all kinds of groups on all kinds of issues. Each time I have seen that the power of all the groups working together

1

was greater than that of each group acting alone. But I operated intuitively, sometimes using the force of my personality, rather than implementing a systematic practice that could be passed along to others. Gradually, however, I have developed a Trans-organizational System (TS) model that works, and which I want to share with others.

With this book I want to show activists and change agents how this form of organization can help them achieve their goals in a way they could not do alone. I provide an explanation of the TS and how it works. Drawing on a variety of theories, models, and frameworks, I have attached names to different parts of the form and have identified pertinent issues or questions.

I want to make it clear that we cannot develop TSs using the same methods we employ with traditional organizations (non-profits included). Because of the unique attributes of the multi-organization form, we have to operate differently. In this book, I present a framework of tools and processes TS conveners and developers can use to develop TSs from scratch. If we follow this model, we may still make mistakes as we create multi-organization alliances, but we should make far fewer!

I have written this book:

- to give insight into trans-organizational processes and why we are using them,
- to provide a trans-organizational development model,
- to give an understanding of power relations in this form of organization,
- to provide a model of organizational effectiveness,
- to explore horizontal boundaries between member organizations,
- to present tools for trans-organizational development, and
- to stimulate the acquisition of the leadership skills necessary for this form of organization.

How Did I Come to Write This Book?

Like most of my generation, I came to trans-organizational systems by a circuitous path. I studied political science in my undergraduate years and went on to spend much of my adult life on one political campaign after another. Alliances among groups are crucial in these campaigns, so this organizational form — an organization of organizations — was something I knew about in a political sense.

As an activist and organizer, I found that partnerships and alliances were natural tools to use to achieve social justice and community development objectives. Representatives from disparate advocacy groups would come together and form a new group with autonomous and usually short-term goals. We displayed our political strength by drafting letters of support listing the names of all our origi-nating organizations. It was an impressive way to show the numbers supporting our cause. Beyond this, I knew little about applying the idea of multi-organiza-tional alliances to my day-to-day work as an activist and community developer. I understood that when one party lacks resources, partnering with another who has what you lack makes common sense. But I found little direction or guidance from academics or from other organization developers on how to do so.

Eventually I went back to school for a masters degree focusing on organiza-tional development and learned about making traditional organizations work better. For my thesis project I undertook an intervention (organization develop-ers use the term "intervention" to describe a process designed to improve group functioning) with a multistakeholder organization that had been coming together to work on various projects for over 30 years. At that point it operated mainly as a network, with members sharing information about each other's services, but without any common goals or purpose. Without the benefit of a body of aca-demic research describing optimal trans-organizational functioning and effective change TS processes, I did what I needed to fit the masters program require-ments and led a strategic planning process that produced goals and strategies for the organization, but I left the project feeling there was much more that needed to be done in terms of dealing with the organizational structure and underlying power issues.

Unsure exactly what was required, I decided to find the answers in and through my own experience creating TSs and dealing with dysfunction. I was fin-ished school, but I looked, as always, to whatever discipline could provide me with insight and tools. The field of organizational development provided some answers, but my informal study and reading in politics, governance, and day-to-day admin-istration also provided concepts and tools to facilitate the development of new complex structures needed to solve the difficult issues my TSs were addressing.

I didn't have the answers, or even many of the questions, assembled into a coherent model at the time, but I began to formulate the questions that, through additional research, interdisciplinary study, and practice, came to form the basis of the development model in this book.

In the 1990s I was elected to the city council of York, Ontario, a municipality in bad shape after a corruption scandal and economic restructuring that left the community without its traditional industrial tax base. The rest of the province was also suffering high unemployment and recession, and as the provincial govern-ment was unable to give much help, the only recourse was to reorganize and revi-talize the local economy by using existing resources. This could only happen by pulling together the various players in the local economy and steering them all in the same direction. As the chair of the city's land use committee, responsible for local economic development and urban planning, I argued for this course of action and found all other council members on side. They were supportive, but at the same time they did not allocate any funding when they passed a motion empowering me to run with the idea.

Despite the challenges, the multistakeholder Community Economic Development Advisory Committee for the City of York, which became known as CEDAC, was born. CEDAC was made up of city bureaucrats and politicians, businesspeople, non-profit staff, and cultural groups. It did everything from citywide strategic planning to advocacy with other levels of government, and it supported a number of program initiatives that mobilized the community around a common vision. I was involved in the process for over three years, working on it for at least two hours of every working day. I call it a process because it was initially a planning process under the umbrella of city government. It became a TS when the plan moved into its implementation phase and resources, decision making, and work activity started to be shared amongst TS members. Those hours devoted to CEDAC activity were filled with meetings, decision making, capacity building, politicking, and hand holding — the day-to-day work that is necessary to help a multistakeholder process realize its desired outcomes.

CEDAC was eventually used as a model by the federal government to revitalize a number of other neighborhoods in Toronto after the City of York was amalgamated into the new City of Toronto in 1998. In 1997 I wrote about the process that led to CEDAC for the Caledon Institute for Social Policy. In my article I attributed CEDAC's success to the following factors:

+ Involving stakeholders from different sectors
+ Investing limited funding strategically
+ Encouraging an open discussion of divergent points of view
+ Developing a common understanding of the problem
+ Developing a common vision using a neutral facilitator
+ Appointing coordinators for the various functions

I have since been involved in many successful collaborative processes and want to share the knowledge I developed along the way. This book identifies the day-to-day practices that make a TS work.

Who is this Book For?

This book is a how-to guide. It will help multistakeholder groups and their principle champions create an effective trans-organizational system from day one. It illustrates why this form of organization is developing at this time and how interorganizational collaboration can address complicated problems and move complex systems. It provides a developmental framework and a process model for organizational effectiveness that incorporates governance, people, and coordination tools in order to activate and sustain the TS.

I have written the book with the following readers in mind:

- Community and social workers
- Health promoters
- Government program staff, particularly those in municipal government, land use, and health and social services
- Staff of professional associations
- Non-profit agency executive directors
- Economic development officers
- Crime prevention and law enforcement workers
- International development workers

I anticipate that these readers are members, coordinators, and leaders of their organizations and are struggling through inter-organizational collaboration efforts. The book contains tools for these organizational pioneers' most critical needs, such as selecting members, developing a vision, building trust, creating and running meetings, and supporting the ongoing work, and I expect they will find it dog-eared as they refer to it again and again to guide them through their development process.

My experience is primarily in non-profits, so my anecdotes and examples come from that sector. My research includes the literature for the fields of organization development, management science, and health promotion. However, the theoretical frameworks, tools, and models would also benefit those engaged in building strategic alliances in the private sector.

What are Alliances, Coalitions, and Partnerships?

Organizational theory uses the term *system* to describe an organization of people who come together for a common purpose. A crowd in the subway is not a system, but a family is.

The form of organization represented by my catchall title *Alliances, Coalitions and Partnerships* is an interorganizational system that has become semi-autonomous but maintains accountability and feedback loops to its organizations of origin. Thomas Cummings, an organizational development theorist, labeled this type of organization a trans-organizational system, or TS, in a 1984 article he wrote for the journal *Research in Organizational Behaviour*. I have adopted it as the generic term for this type of organization throughout this book.

The building block for this type of organization is not the person but the organization. The originating organizations maintain a vested interest in the outcome and day-to-day activity of the new TS.

What is a TS used for?

The TS form of organization often happens in the "space" between traditional organizations and macro systems like society or government or community. It is a response to the problem of organizational silos, in which each group is looking out only for its own interests (see Figure I.1).

I.1: *Space between the silos*

Gary Nelson, in his book *Self Governance in Communities and Families*, says that as more people feel farther removed from government and reject the politics of manipulation that they believe are practiced by mainstream political parties, they are finding in the space between government and existing institutions a vacuum that can be filled with local nongovernment leadership. In this case, a TS can build a community consensus on issues and provide a mechanism for community mobilization and eventually self-governance. It is a rare politician who will not support a community consensus.

There are many other uses for a TS. It can be a tool to mobilize for social change or to modify the behavior of large groups of people for improved health outcomes or other community interests. It can build broad-based consensus on how to tackle issues like substance abuse or economic revitalization.

TSs can also be used as part of a strategy to build large-scale support to offset the power and intransigence of established systems like bureaucracies. They provide a consensus-building process that is useful for politicians who want to react to new expressions of political will but fear alienating existing support. This is critical, as systemic change can only happen when the players in the system all start making decisions in concert with an agreed-upon course of action.

A TS can be the remedy for haphazard government or non-profit delivery systems that evolved from "flavor of the month" public priorities and now need to be rationalized to respond to current realities. When they undergo unplanned growth, many human service systems are fragmented into several autonomous organizations, each responsible for a small piece of the whole program. Overall coordination rarely exists. This fragmentation is now seen as part of the problem.

The rallying cry from government and funders is that coordination of existing services can bring benefits to the user through one-stop shopping and case management services. It can also benefit the provider by preventing the duplication of human services and by freeing up resources to serve greater numbers in more creative ways.

The private sector often uses the term *joint venture* to describe two or more organizations coming together in some way to maximize efficiency and opportunity. Joint ventures are also TSs. They combine knowledge and resources to create some form of added value for their existing product or service line. For example, two companies might combine the best of a skilled local workforce with foreign technology.

TSs are becoming the vehicle of choice for health promotion. Research shows that the best health promotion initiatives are those that intervene simultaneously at different levels, including the individual, family, school, and community. A TS integrates all the players to collaborate and develop a multifaceted response to the issue. Community-based partnerships can mobilize individuals and institutions to address a particular aspect of the problem or to combine their resources to create integrated prevention programming.

Why are they so important?

Most often, TSs are considered a tool by organizations responsible for long-term community development. When I speak of TSs as a *tool*, I mean that they are something we use to perform our occupation or profession. If you are a health promoter, I probably do not need to tell you that TSs are a tool you can use to produce better health outcomes in your community. Others may consider the TS a *strategy* — a long-term plan of action for achieving a specific vision or set of goals.

> The trans-organizational system can be both a tool and a strategy.

- A TS can be a tool to deal with turbulence and complexity in the environment through active adaptation and systems change.
- A TS can be a tool to mobilize the political power of interorganizational collaboration. It is an effective organizational form for lobbying purposes. Anti-smoking bylaws are the successful outcome of community-based advocacy coalitions.
- Often a TS is the only way (i.e., a strategy) to revitalize a stagnant system and introduce efficiency into fragmented service delivery systems.
- A TS is the most effective vehicle to create and disseminate a new vision and direction for a large-scale system such as a community, a business or government

sector, or an industry. It is often the strategy of choice for community-academic partnerships working to bridge the gap between end users and academics.

+ As a strategy, a TS is often the best way to create change in the broader world outside a community, crossing regional or national boundaries. For instance, in the international campaign against land mines, non-governmental organizations (NGOs), governments, and celebrities combined forces to raise awareness of the issue, advocate for a policy framework, secure resources, and develop a delivery infrastructure to address the issue. This, in effect, is a TS.

What is this Book About?

This book describes the steps managers, coordinators, and practitioners might take to develop effective multistakeholder processes and organizations — what I am calling trans-organizational systems. Often when people begin to establish such an organization, they must act quickly to achieve the group's purpose. The result is that action preempts the work of developing structure and capacity that will sustain the organization in the longer term. I address this problem in Chapter 1 with an overview of today's social and political context, in which TSs are becoming the preferred organizational form for actively adapting to complexity and rapid change.

Chapter 2 presents the TS form of organization, while Chapter 3 provides an overview of a development framework for TSs. Some TSs entrench themselves as permanent fixtures, while others formalize projects or arrangements through partnership contracts. My experience has been that unless a TS is created solely to plan one event or develop a policy, it almost always takes two to four years to achieve its objectives and successfully complete its task. In that time frame, the leadership, staff, and even membership will often change. Therefore, people must construct systems of organizational memory in order to pass along the purpose, objectives, and history of the TS.

Chapter 4 explores the issue of power in a TS, including the particular form of TS governments use for consulting about policy. Chapter 5 presents a model for organizational effectiveness that incorporates the process streams of trust-building, governance, and management. All three process streams are equally important and critical to developing a flexible structure and creating a sustainable TS that will fulfill its purpose. This chapter provides the reader with an understanding of each type of process intervention and why it is used at that particular point in development. Later chapters include specific tools to meet the particular process needs at each stage of development.

Chapters 6 through 8 further elaborate the organizational effectiveness model by presenting practical tools and conceptual models you can use when creating the organizational infrastructure of a TS. Chapter 9 discusses the need for unique leadership skills in this form of organization, what I am calling *lateral leadership*. In Chapter 10 I take the reader back to my first TS — CEDAC — and walk through its development, identifying the steps and processes used and (with the grace of hindsight) suggesting what might have been done to improve the ultimate sustainability of the process. Chapter 11 presents some of the questions I am frequently asked at workshops and suggests some future areas for research. Throughout the book I will explore what academics and theoreticians have contributed to understanding the unique nature of this form of organization.

I have structured this book in a linear fashion, although I realize not many TSs have developed in the same manner! However, the processes and tools are not intended to be used in linear time, but as intervention choices whenever deemed appropriate. Some TSs have been formed at the end of the development framework presented in Chapter 3 and just cycle around to the beginning. Some TSs need a lot of structure; others need little. This book is not a definitive guide, but a starting point for all the organizational pioneers taking on the challenges of our time by building this new form of organization.

CHAPTER 1

The Context and Societal Drivers

Living is a form of not being sure, not knowing what next or how. The moment
you know how, you begin to die a little. The artist never entirely knows. We
guess. We may be wrong, but we take leap after leap in the dark.

Agnes de Mille

There is an Old Jewish saying: "Oy vey, to have such problems!" I often envision my forebears uttering such words. I suspect my starving ancestors, living in damp hovels, pressed into service as indentured servants or as unwilling members of Her Majesty's navy, would switch places with me anytime. Unending hot water, instant meals, fresh fruit year-round, central heat and air-conditioning, and still we complain. Most people in North America lead lives of luxury compared to those of our ancestors. Yet some of the things they took for granted have disappeared from our modern lives — concepts and traditions like cooperation, taking care of one's own, day-to-day routine, a close connection to nature, and an awareness of nature's abundance.

The Context: Disengagement and Isolation

Now we are global citizens who need filters to mediate the information explosion. "Too much information," we cry. We are inundated by messages and directives telling us not how to be or how to act, but only to *buy*. Our lifestyles are built upon what we buy and what brands we identify with. Those at the lower end of the income scale are relegated to transient jobs with increasingly lower wages,[1] but people seem to be able to keep buying, and as long as they get more stuff and more "toys" they remain complacent. The media have become a tool that trains the citizenry for passivity. In the 19th century, Marx said religion was the opiate of the masses. Many are now saying TV, electronic games, and pornography are the opiate of the 21st century.[2]

While we now have the best-educated population in the history of the world, academics like Thomas Homer-Dixon have identified that our ever-increasing

11

systemic complexity has created an "ingenuity gap" — "the critical gap between our need for ideas to solve complex problems and our actual supply of those ideas." Years of socialization to accommodate the workforce needs of industrial manufacturing have created a regimented, fearful, subservient human being.[3] Even when we are not in a strictly controlled, rules-based organization, internalized oppression from our existing hierarchical organizations means we do not have the skills to be high-performing, autonomous workers and citizens. As a result, we are unable to solve the serious problems currently facing humankind.

The manipulation of TV news and the endless propaganda of social marketing create a fear-based culture filled with people who are terrified that something bad will happen if they leave their homes or develop a sore throat.[4] We are told by endless advertisers and so-called experts that the world is our village now, but at the same time many adults don't have any friends. According to the *Utne Reader* of November 2001, the average American spends nine years watching television. To compensate, health promoters devise disease-prevention strategies that involve developing social support systems for our at-risk populations, but in a 1999 report, "Toward a Healthy Future," Health Canada pointed out that having friends and a support network is one of the determinants of health.

This disassociation and isolation of our population also translates into high rates of addiction and depression.[5] Not surprisingly, this situation allows pharmaceutical companies to make billions from "lifestyle" drugs such as Prozac, Viagra, and diet pills, and politicians use fear-based messages to win election. Disengagement from the propaganda grid may be the most logical and effective strategy to preserve our mental health, but this often leads to political disengagement as well.

Political disengagement often results from the fact that, in today's world, celebrity seems to be the primary criteria for leadership. To many citizens, all politicians seem to be impotent, which leaves voters to endure the tyranny of empty choice at the ballot box. In the age of mass media, those who select candidates look for their TV quotient (TVQ), which includes how they look on TV and how often they have appeared on TV, because it is through TV exposure that most voters decide who to vote for. As a municipal politician, I did not need a TVQ, but when I ran for a nomination at the provincial (state) level of government, I learned that was the criteria by which I was judged. It didn't matter what I had accomplished for my community or how I brought people together. As a result, I lost the nomination.

The trend of amalgamating governments and local institutions, which creates more distance between the government and the governed,[6] also leads to political disengagement. There is a widespread attitude of entitlement among the citizenry of western countries, but the corresponding sense of responsibility is on the decline. Voter turnouts for elections continue to drop, and non-profit organizations report declining numbers of volunteers. Advertising and even some political leaders constantly send the message that the highest and best use of citizens' time and money is to keep the economy going — which they can do by shopping. For example, after the events of September 11, 2001, the US president exhorted Americans to get back into the shopping malls. In early 2003, Toronto was hit by an epidemic of severe acute respiratory syndrome (SARS), and the local politicians were no different. They encouraged community action to beat the epidemic by urging everyone to get the economy rolling again, to go shopping or eat out.

Meanwhile, opportunities for people to engage as citizens or community members are becoming rare. Instead of public meetings, governments have implemented "e-government," adopting the Internet as an efficient vehicle for public opinion consultation. There is no need to have face-to-face time with citizens or for citizens to engage with one another. In my province, the amalgamation of human-sized communities into mega-cities effectively eliminated participation in local governance by eliminating the level of government closest to the people.

As a result of information overload, the emphasis on consumerism, and the flood of electronic toys with somnolent effects, citizens are not noticing this process and are therefore colluding in it. By colluding we have given up much of what it means to be happy and healthy humans. According to the major world philosophers and religions, the following values make us healthy and happy humans:

- A balance of work and play
- A sense of spirituality and connection to nature
- Living with family and in community
- Experiencing beauty through nature, art, dancing, and singing

But when do we ever receive instruction or messages from our culture about these fundamental characteristics of a well-lived human life? Instead we are encouraged to work nonstop to achieve personal economic objectives, like becoming a millionaire before age 40. We are persuaded to purchase consumer products that destroy our natural environment. We leave behind community and often family in the quest for the materialist "good life," while beauty can only be experienced through the mediation of a professional artist. It is rare in North American society that people engage in art, singing, or dancing *on a regular basis* just for the sheer joy of it.

Our collusion is a defense mechanism and survival technique that allows the current social order to persist for a time until it reforms or implodes. While most of the population of the West remains in a state of passivity, our society faces chronic problems, including increasing poverty in both the first and developing worlds, inequality, social breakdown, and global environmental catastrophes.[7]

Ironically, by our disengagement we have given up the chance to solve these complex social and environmental problems. It is clear that to deal with such issues as crime, substance abuse, economic revitalization, and others, we need to engage all citizens — parents and politicians, public servants and entrepreneurs — and get them to work together. Isolation and disengagement do not contribute to the solution, but participation and engagement do. Organizing ourselves to deal with these ills and with alienation is not only the strategy to find solutions to these problems, but also, in the process of engagement with one another, is a chance for us to find our humanity.

Collaboration is the key to finding solutions in every case. People couldn't overthrow an autocratic monarchy or dictatorship until they all started working together in a democracy. The same thing happens with TSs — problems seem insurmountable, but when people and groups start collaborating, they can achieve more.

Societal Drivers

Societal drivers are the principal causes of broad-based social change. Academics observe social trends and then analyze what factors led to the observed change. Usually the same causal factors (causes) lead to many different forms of social change. If those causal factors have an impact on many different areas, they are called societal drivers. The main factors driving social change today are:

- Technology and the inter-networked enterprise
- Our current turbulent environment
- The opportunity of adaptive space
- Flatter, more democratic organizations
- Social capital that fills the ingenuity gap
- More effective government

Technology and the inter-networked enterprise

The principal driver enabling the development of the TS is information technology. Organizations, businesses, homes, and consumers can now connect via the Internet. Broadcast e-mails can transmit all sorts of information quickly and efficiently.

From a macroeconomic perspective, every individual enterprise is part of an interlinked business "ecosystem," with each link dependent in one way or another on the others.[8] Just-in-time production and supply chains in the auto industry are a good example of this, as auto parts manufacturers lay off their staff in line with layoffs of their customers, the big automakers.

From a business perspective, inter-networked enterprise gives companies the ability to configure and manage themselves in a way that best suits their business goals and the desires of their partners and customers. From an organizational development perspective, the ability to collect and share information outside the organization has allowed many new forms of cooperation and collaboration to evolve. The network structure emerged as a way to share information across boundaries previously thought to be impermeable. The technology has allowed partners to work together with minimal structure, but we are still inventing new forms and methods of collaboration.

Networked computers not only support the function of a new form of organization, but they also provide a new organizational model, a web or circular network model (see Figure 1.1), in place of the hierarchical triangle with concentrated power and authority at the top, which is the common form of most of our institutions.

1.1: *Networked computers are the metaphor for networked organizations.*

As we observed the computer-networking capabilities provided by the Internet, we applied the same logic to our organizations. If computers could be networked, we realized other systems could be, as well, such as supply chains in businesses and the one-stop-shopping model for social services.

Our current turbulent environment

In their Open Systems theory, Eric Trist and Fred Emery present four environments that human society has adapted to over the past 5,000 years. Their model, outlined in Figure 1.2, provides a lens through which we can understand our current environment.[9]

We are currently in a Type IV environment of constant turbulence. Competitive pressures on industry and workforces due to the global marketplace make it a challenging time in which to live and work. The pace of change and innovation is without precedent in human history. Our political (and economic) realities include random terrorist attacks and the possibility of large-scale biological warfare. Nearly two years after the events of September 11, 2001, Osama bin Laden, the alleged mastermind behind the attacks on the World Trade Center and the

Pentagon, is still at large, likely living in a lawless, primitive land connected electronically to a TS called al-Qaeda. Russell Ackoff, one of the originators of systems thinking, calls the intractable problems we face in our chaotic environment "meta-problems" and "messes."[10]

1.2: *Changing Human Environments*

Type 1 (Before 3500 BC)

- Random pattern of human settlement and organization
- Hunter-gatherer systems

The hunter-gatherer society was based on tribal organization. Competition for herds and prime fishing and nut- and fruit-gathering territory led to localized conflict. Societal organization was easily uprooted and moved.

Type II (3500 BC-AD 1750)

- Placid, clustered pattern of human settlement and organization
- Agricultural-based society
- Cooperation is the organizing principle for human systems at all levels.

This environment became the catalyst for human culture to develop. A broader based tribe or clan structure led to the formation of towns and cities.

Type III (AD 1750-1950)

- Disturbed reactive pattern of human settlement and organization
- Industrial-based society brutally imposed upon people tied to the land
- Competition becomes the organizing principle for human systems
- Problem solving is the focus for coming together for collective learning
- Organizational strategy is direct, with a push through obstacles and a focus on short-term wins
- Principle assumption for organization planning is that there is an endpoint and you can design the means to reach it

This is the industrial revolution and the modern age. Energy sources are harnessed and united with technology to produce constant technical innovation. Capitalism and nation-states are developed to accommodate this technological innovation.

Type IV (1950-present)

- A turbulent pattern of human settlement and organization
- Knowledge-based society experiencing rapid value shifts, uncertainties, discontinuities
- Co-opetition (a combination of competition and cooperation) becomes the organizing principle for human organization
- Puzzle learning is the focus for coming together for collective learning and knowledge transformation

- Organizational strategy is indirect, focused on the art of maneuvering, with long time frames
- Principle assumption for organization planning is that you start by setting an endpoint that reflects shared ideals

This is our current environment, a transition from the modern industrial economy to an information economy operating on a global scale. A global value system and organizational forms (except for multinational corporations) are not yet developed. Widespread suffering occurs due to displacement from human-scale institutions such as family, church, and nation-states.

Existing institutions and processes are often stalemated and unable to respond to new realities of globalization.

To address these messes and meta-problems we must shift from the level of the single organization to the population of organizations that share a concern for these problems. This "organizational ecology" perspective[11] aims to draw together a wide range of social organizations in order to develop a multi-organizational response to meta-problems. Even the superpower United States could not act unilaterally to deal with al-Qaeda, but needed the support of its global neighbors.

In our Type IV environment, rapid decision making is necessary in order to adapt to rapid change. But the issues to be decided are often extremely complex. To make it easier to deal with this complexity and the uncertainties and new responses of others, we need multiple inputs. The intelligence or knowledge found in single organizations is often inadequate.

To actively adapt to the turbulent environment, independent organizations are motivated to seek expertise and capacity beyond what they themselves can produce. The intelligence gathering and sharing of many organizations can provide the additional knowledge needed to produce a more effective response to a set of problems such as homelessness or poverty. The shared capacity and resources of housing, counseling, and education providers can produce a more effective program to address poverty, for example, than any one agency or type of intervention operating alone.

New forms of organization have developed in order to adapt to meta-problems. Like federated states, we now have federated organizations at the grassroots level of service delivery and health prevention. When one organization cannot solve a problem, a popular alternative is to look for other organizations to partner with and create a solution. These solution-focused configurations are multiparty organizations or multistakeholder processes and are rooted in a different power dynamic than a traditional organization, which is most often organized along hierarchical lines. Due to the equality inherent in shared responsibility and the power associated with membership, these TSs tend to develop as a more democratic form of organization.

Our Type IV turbulent environment requires a nonlinear and expansive approach to planning when creating a response or strategy. If you think "outside the box," you can also think outside the organization. If you start with the vision of a desired state, then you can work backward, identifying all the necessary ingredients and actions needed to make the desired future a reality. If during the thinking process there are no restrictions on whom or what to use as resources, then you will look beyond the confines of your own organization at other systems or organizations in the environment and seek to collaborate to make the pool of resources larger. Whenever this process occurs — bringing together the resources of more than one organization to achieve a desired end — another higher-level system or organization (a TS) is created to implement the agreed-upon response or strategy.

A major benefit of interorganizational collaboration is that the turbulent environment is calmed as the TS responds and adapts to the messes in the environment. Figure 1.3 shows the relationship of a single organization with its environment, while Figure 1.4 illustrates the impact that the formation of a TS

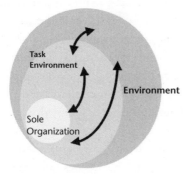

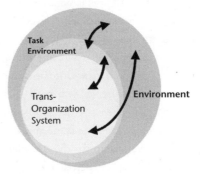

1.3: *Sole organization in its environment*

Every organization exists within an environment. An environment contains everything outside the organization, including all other organizations and the related interactivity. A task environment consists of the organizations and activity happening outside the organization related to the work of the sole organization. Therefore, activities in the task environment will likely have more impact on the organization.

1.4: *Trans-organizational system in its environment*

If a sole organization joins with other organizations to create a trans-organizational system, more of the environment comes under the influence of the new TS. The turbulence caused by complex problems in the environment . can be addressed by the consolidated resources and knowledge base of the new TS. The span of the TS covers considerably more than the single organization in Figure 1.3 did.

can have on its task environment. The TS's greater influence over the environment further calms the turbulence.

The opportunity of adaptive space

At present there is widespread consciousness of emerging forms of organization. Until recently, the mechanistic or machine-like form of organization was the most accepted organizational metaphor throughout the Western world. Fredrick Taylor's conceptual model of bureaucratizing work and dividing labor into standardized pieces (like a machine) influenced all forms of organization from business to recreation and the family.[12]

For the longest time, human beings were considered interchangeable parts or cogs in the machinelike organization. This type of organization, and the unthinking worker it required, is no longer the predominant model in the post-industrial economies of the western world. Theories in quantum physics and biology have been translated into concepts like self-organizing systems and are becoming popular in organizational development theory. Innovation is seen as the key to an ever-expanding economy. One must think in order to innovate. Therefore, a thinking human worker is now perceived as an asset. Managers need to continue the core work of the organization without assuming limitless expansion of the core work or product line, but at the same time they need to innovate and develop new products or services to maintain growth. If they cannot expand the core business or silo, the opportunity for change and growth lies in the spaces between the silos. Each silo can continue to do what it does best, but in order to remain relevant, innovative, and adaptive, managers must look to the space outside the silo (see Figure 1.5).

1.5: *Adaptive space is found between the silos*

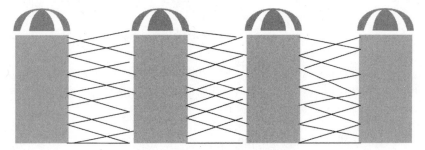

By the late 20th century, the silo-like organizations found that they always needed to grow, but there was an other option for growth: the trans-organizational system. By moving activity outside the organizational boundary and partnering with other oganizations, new business operations could operate in the previously empty space between autonomous organizations.

TSs are what emerge in the adaptive spaces. A merger would collapse two silos into each other. However, by participating in a TS, the silos can collaborate with others to develop innovative solutions to the problem sets in their environment while maintaining their independence. Trans-organizational systems represent the evolution of higher, more responsive organizational forms from less complex structures.

Flatter, more democratic organizations

The trend toward flatter organizations, and the value of pushing decision making down to the levels where the work is done, are now accepted as good doctrine, if not necessarily implemented in practice. It is no longer desirable to use control mechanisms to supervise professional workers, who in many cases know more about the work than their supervisors. Instead, performance indicators are used to assess worker output. This lessening of control is necessary to encourage creativity and innovation and leads to more participative and democratic workplaces, which in turn attract and retain creative, autonomous workers.

In order to maximize their talent and skill sets, the more highly educated workers in today's organizations need a different socialization and education process than the regimented assembly-line workers that dominated our previous industrial economy. This poses new challenges for the way our society is organized. For instance, the factory-based schools of the 20th century do not churn out confident, creative workers but docile and compliant ones. If we need an autonomous worker capable of making decisions, our school system and cultural norms need to change to support that. Our economy is demanding a different kind of human, but we are not yet producing the schooling and the workplace that supports the kind of individual growth needed for the high-performing organization. This is emerging as one of the key business issues of the 21st century.

I have often heard from managers that a TS provides the kind of democratic, supportive environment in which workers can experiment with autonomy and decision-making responsibilities. By its democratic nature, a TS can provide fertile ground for the kind of personal development that workers can transfer back to their organizations of origin.

Social capital fills the ingenuity gap

Social capital has been described as "A combination of the elements of mutual trust, reciprocity, group belongingness, the collective sense of a shared future, and collective action."[13] Social capital is also the outcome of a successful TS. For example, when various actors and systems that make up a community or sector collaborate and cooperate to address their "meta-problems and messes," then the community's or sector's capacity to address its own problems is developed. In another example, entrepreneurial initiatives are built on mutual trust among the players. If they are successful, that trust will remain and perhaps lead to further initiatives.

A plan that is developed through the collaboration of community members is also more likely to be sustainable over the long term than a government report written and developed by expert outsiders. In Chapter 10, I describe my experience on York city council when we hired an expert consultant to create an economic development strategy, but had neither the resources nor the money to implement the recommendations. A year or two later, when we initiated a community-based planning process, we unleashed the resources and energy of many decision makers, including ourselves as city councilors, city staff, other levels of government, and the non-profit sector. Amazing things happened because, through the process, participants co-developed the vision, understood the reason for proposed changes, and desired the benefits of change. The vision, collective understanding, and trust generated by the process became the motivation behind the new road map for change.

More effective government

Governments are often in the forefront of encouraging the development of TSs, and government representatives are often willing to participate in or fund the formation of a TS. Governments interested in forming trans-organization systems are driven by the need to:

- Reduce the cost and role of government in order to economize and use government funds for leverage
- Increase the effectiveness of programming in order to undertake system planning and rationalizing, and to produce outputs more in tune with the needs of the groups they are supposed to serve
- Improve public policy in order to avoid costly mistakes and produce outputs that match the needs of users by involving service providers and end users in the design and development of policy and programming[14]

The formation of TSs are a response to the challenges of our times. While the development of information technology has changed the way we relate to each other as human beings and is presenting incredible challenges to human social systems, the underlying geometric configuration of the technology itself — the web or circle — is becoming the metaphor from which we are creating new organizational forms in order to respond to the complex challenges of our times.

CHAPTER 2

The Trans-Organizational System of Organization

If we value independence, if we are disturbed by the growing conformity of knowledge, of values, of attitudes, which our present system induces, then we may wish to set up conditions of learning which make for uniqueness, for self-direction, and for self-initiated learning.

Carl Rogers

In the previous chapter we learned that it is prudent to collaborate with other organizations in order to adapt to the turbulence in our environments. This chapter will describe the development of a single organization and then the development of a multiparty organization in order to illuminate the difference.

What is an Organization?

Organizations (often called systems) are structures of human relationships designed to achieve goals through work. Even if these goals are focused on recreation or a family, there are clear boundaries, well-defined roles, and the assumption of authority by, or delegation of authority to, individuals or subgroups in order to achieve an organization's primary task or mission.

Organizations are *socio-technical systems* — in other words, social as well as technical systems. *Technical* refers to the aspect of the organization that is developed to facilitate work, while *social* refers to the way social relationships facilitate (or fail to facilitate) the work.

Organizations often develop "social defenses" — structures, procedures, and informal delegations — that help participants cope with anxieties linked to both work and relationships. At times, such defenses can seem rational, even necessary, as group members relate to "the way things have always been done." At other times these defenses and their emotional subtext impede the completion of tasks and goals and strain relationships. This emotional undercurrent in a group or

23

organization often stymies the best of intentions and the most rational of tasks. Ignore the social system and you might watch your organization die.

What kind of work do organizations do?

Organizations must have a *system principle*, a reason for being. In the case of a family, this principle can be providing emotional and financial support for, and/or raising, children. In the case of a non-profit organization, the mission is to provide service or education. In a business, the system principle is the provision of goods or services for profit.

Organizations manage knowledge to achieve desired results. Knowledge is a critical mass of information, looked at through the lens of experience and critical thinking, which enables us to predict and control something. Organizations are made up of knowledge specialists and generalists. Generalists take the specialists' knowledge and communicate it to other specialists, who add their particular value to the knowledge. Bits of knowledge by themselves are sterile. They become productive only if welded together into a single unified body of knowledge.

According to Peter Drucker in *Post-Capitalist Society*, making this transformation of knowledge possible is the organization's task, the reason for its existence or its function.[1] In other words, the work of the organization is to add value to incoming information gleaned from its workers, its customers/clients, and its environment and then transform this enhanced information into the output of a service or product. If there is no value-added process or transformation, there is no work and no authentic organization. In the case of a family, the transformation of knowledge results in meeting the needs of family members, emotionally as well as financially.

Organizations as specialized bodies of knowledge

Knowledge specialists have evolved from the craftsperson of the Middle Ages. Medieval craftspeople learned their craft from a master and, after many years of practice, taught what they knew to apprentices. The knowledge was contained in the brain of one and passed along to another. Once that body of knowledge could be systematically recorded, it was possible to pass it on to the next generation without long apprenticeships. A *methodology* converts a *craft* into a *discipline* — for example, applying quantitative methodology or the scientific method to the craft of building construction turned the craft of constructing buildings into the discipline of engineering. Methodologies convert ad hoc experience into a system of knowledge by transforming anecdotes into information, skills into something that can be taught and learned.[2]

When an organization possesses a body of knowledge that it uses to adapt to complex problem sets or messes (or to provide goods and services for a market), that body of knowledge is unique to that organization. This specialized organizational knowledge is now a knowledge resource similar to the body of knowledge that is passed on during an engineering degree program.

We have a complex society that suffers from information overload. Each one of us seeks to discern what we need to know or do to meet the requirements of any given moment. We don't have time or room for duplication of information or knowledge. With Internet technology we can efficiently distribute information to just about anyone. But the creation of knowledge involves adding value to that information. An organization that serves a particular niche is its knowledge specialist. We should consider organizations as repositories of specialized knowledge or as knowledge specialists in the same way lawyers and engineers are knowledge specialists.

What is a Trans-Organizational System?

Trans-organizational systems (TSs) are organizations too. They must meet the criteria specified above for organizations, including having a system principle and transforming knowledge by adding value. As organizations of organizations, they are functional social systems existing in the space between single organizations and societal systems such as government. They are able to make decisions and perform tasks on behalf of their member organizations, while the member organizations maintain their separate identities and goals. According to Thomas G. Cummings and Christopher G. Worley in *Organization Development and Change*:

> In contrast to most organizations, TSs tend to be underorganized; relationships among organizations are loosely coupled; leadership and power are dispersed among autonomous organizations, rather than hierarchically centralized; and commitment and membership are tenuous as member organizations attempt to maintain their autonomy while jointly performing.[3]

What kind of work do trans-organizational systems do?

A trans-organizational system also manages knowledge. A TS must be managed in a similar fashion to any organization comprised of specialists. But in a TS, the member organizations hold the specialized knowledge and participate in the process as the voices of the knowledge specialists. The specialist knowledge is not necessarily the knowledge of an academic discipline, but can also be the voice of a particular constituency's lived experience. It depends on the problem set that is motivating the formation of a TS.

The TS must bridge the specialist identities and accountabilities of member organizations in order to produce new knowledge that allows those organizations to adapt to or change the turbulent environment. This does not preclude a TS having individual members, but TSs are primarily made up of people from groups representing various constituencies that have a voice in the process.

In the development of a TS, the boundaries can be ambiguous for a long time. The group and the structure are co-created through process and dialogue. Power is shared among the organizations of origin. Within the TS, information flows horizontally between member organizations as opposed to vertically. Clearly, a TS needs a different form of structure than is found in hierarchical organizations in order to facilitate work and information flow.

The culture of a TS may incorporate the cultures of originating organizations, or an entirely new culture can emerge. It all depends on the conscious or unconscious decisions TS members make about values, beliefs, and assumptions. These decisions form and influence the emotional undercurrent I mentioned earlier.

What kinds of organizations are TSs?

In order to define the types of organizations that can legitimately be labeled TSs, we might place multiparty organizations along a continuum that ranges from the loosest form of collaboration, on the left of the diagram in Figure 2.1, to the tightest.

At the looser end of the spectrum are *coalitions*. They usually have the least structure, often relying only on terms of reference and a decision-making process, and are apt to be used for advocacy purposes. In that case, they forgo a vision development process in favor of a process for reaching agreement on objectives on an advocacy strategy. *Coalition* is a term favored by health promoters for a TS aimed at achieving common goals. (Health promoters also use the term *network*,

2.1: *Continuum from the loosest to tightest collaborative structure.*

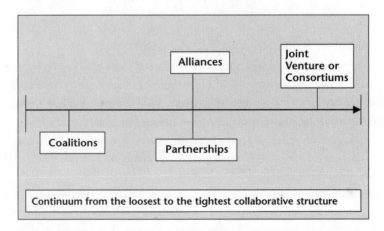

Continuum from the loosest to the tightest collaborative structure

but this creates a mental model of only sharing knowledge and can set up the expectation that no decisions are made.)

A little less loose, perhaps, are *partnerships*, which Barry Oshry, author of *Seeing Systems*, defines as "A relationship in which we are jointly committed to the success of whatever process we are in." The term is particularly favored by government and can include anything from organized consultation processes to service delivery partnerships controlled by contractual agreement.

Generally, business uses the term *strategic alliance*, which also falls about midway on the continuum. (Businesses avoid using the term "partnership" because of its legal use to describe a business partnership, which denotes a corporation and legal framework.) A strategic alliance involves at least two partner firms that remain legally independent after the alliance is formed; share benefits and managerial control over the performance of assigned tasks; and make continuing contributions in one or more strategic areas, such as technology or products.[4] Some non-profit TSs also use the term *alliance* when a TS is formed to explore an issue, advocate, or undertake health promotion.

In any of the above situations, once a clear purpose or common goal is identified involving a tightly focused service or a structure to share administrative functions, the organizations need to formalize an agreement regarding partner contributions and commitment of resources. Then the TS is more likely to use the term *joint venture* or *consortium* to describe the formalized agreement and organizational infrastructure. Partner organizations still remain autonomous, with separate decision-making boards and administration, but the TS is operational to handle a particular business function.

All these forms of TS provide opportunities for mutual collaboration with benefits and results beyond those any single organization or sector could realize alone. They are all organizational options to respond to turbulence in their environments.

Organizations may also respond to environmental turbulence through a *merger*. This is the generic term for a full and final coming together of two previously separate corporations. Legally, mergers often entail one organization (the dissolving corporation) closing and leaving its assets and liabilities to another (the surviving corporation). A merger is *not* a TS, because one of the originating organizations ceases to exist. Where there were two silos before, now there is only one. One silo usually wins the "culture wars," with its corporate culture absorbing the other's, whereas a functional TS must create a combined or new culture.

I have also omitted *networks* from this continuum because when their sole purpose is sharing information, they cannot be considered legitimate TSs. Networks have no system principle (i.e., no transformation of knowledge takes place). A network that is created just to share information among its members does not do

2.2: Matrix of Strategies for Working Together

Type of relationship	Definition	Relationship	Characteristics	Resources	Form of organization
• Networking	• Exchanging information for mutual benefit	• Informal	• Minimal time commitments; Limited levels of trust; No necessity to share turf; Information exchange is the primary focus	• No mutual sharing of resources necessary	• No organization necessary
• Coordinating	• Exchanging information for mutual benefit; Altering activities to achieve a common purpose	• Formal	• Moderate time commitments; Moderate levels of trust; No necessity to share turf; Making access to services or resources more user friendly is the primary focus	• No or minimal mutual sharing of resources necessary	• TS once resources or project management are shared
• Cooperating	• Exchanging information for mutual benefit; Altering activities and sharing resources to achieve a common purpose	• Formal	• Substantial time commitments; High levels of trust; Significant access to each other's turf; Sharing of resources to achieve a common purpose is the primary focus	• Moderate to extensive mutual sharing of resources and some sharing of risks, responsibilities, and rewards	• TS
• Collaborating	• Exchanging information for mutual benefit; Altering activities, sharing resources; and enhancing the capacity of another to achieve a common purpose	• Formal	• Extensive time commitments; Very high levels of trust; Extensive areas of common turf; Enhancing each other's capacity to achieve a common purpose is the primary focus	• Full sharing of resources and full sharing of risks, responsibilities, and rewards	• TS

Based on Himmelman's matrix of strategies, illustrates the range of activities, resources, and characteristics for organizations working together and indicates whether they may be considered TSs.

anything to that input knowledge. Instead, the members are free to take the information away and do with it whatever they choose. There is an assumption that the group makes no decisions and therefore there is no need for accountability. If there is no task or transformation of knowledge, there is no organization. So networks are neither organizations nor TSs.

In saying that networks are not TSs, I am not saying they have no value, just that they are not truly a form of organization. Because there is no task, there is no need to move through a development process and build an infrastructure to support a task. Arthur T. Himmelman, a US consultant, developed a matrix of strategies for working together that helps to distinguish the work of a TS.[5] He characterizes a network as being *informal* as opposed to the *formal* relationship necessary for the higher levels of working together (i.e., coordinating, cooperating, and collaborating). I build on his matrix by saying that the higher levels of working together in fact require the development of a TS to formalize and support the strategy of working together.

I do support using the term "network" to describe a type of organizational structure used by many TSs regardless of whether they are called coalitions, alliances, or partnerships. The network structure is one of the great advances in human organization. It is characterized by its flexibility and adaptability compared to the slow-moving, hierarchically organized, and vertically integrated bureaucratic enterprise. A networked organization moves information and decision making along the horizontal plane inside and outside traditional boundaries, bypassing the bureaucratic practice of moving up and down the approval levels of an isosceles triangle organization chart before action can be taken. The network structure, based on the geometric shape of a circle, is illustrated in Figure 2.3.

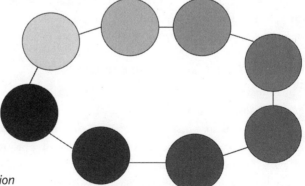

2.3: Network Organization

The organizational structure of a network is a circle, linked on the horizontal axis, as opposed to the vertically linked bureaucratic structure, usually represented by the triangle-shaped organizational chart.

I am frequently asked whether a cross-departmental team is a TS. Although a TS and cross-departmental team can share a similar matrix reporting structure (in matrix management, employees report to both their immediate supervisor and at least one other assigned project manager), the cross-departmental team works within the same organizational structure and culture. The overall organizational mission and culture are the same for all members of the cross-departmental team. All report to the same senior management team, which has the same corporate interests and needs. There is still a need to bridge or overcome boundaries between departments, but they are not as great as those between organizations, so a cross-departmental team is not a TS.

Time frames

No organization lasts forever. But most traditional organizations develop with the assumption that they will be permanent if they are successful at their mission and find an appropriate client/customer base.

This is not the case for TSs. Although the intent may be to develop a long-lasting organization, more often than not organizations forming a TS come together to create something that will achieve a particular objective. A TS seeks to calm environmental turbulence using the combined resources of its organizations of origin. It is temporary in nature, focused on the existing turbulence. At the same time, once a TS is created it can take many years to achieve its objectives and complete what it set out to do. As a result, it may last longer than many new businesses and non-profit organizations.

In practice, TSs are all over the map. They can be temporary organizations or may become a step in an eventual merger of two organizations. In my experience, it takes a while to ascertain the likely time frame, which is intrinsically linked to the vision and strategic planning. All people involved in a TS can do is make sure that they determine time frames when they are developing strategic plans.

Examples of TSs in the non-profit sector

The multistakeholder form of organization makes it possible to join financial and human resources and knowledge in order to understand and solve complex issues whose solutions lie outside the capacity and responsibility of a single player. As stated earlier, TSs can be both a strategy and a tool. The multipartner collaboration of a TS can promote and achieve shared goals in a number of areas — for example, policy, research, planning, program delivery, and funding. These goals may be implemented through myriad activities including advocacy, legislation, community projects, policy planning, and program action. The collaboration may take different forms such as cooperative initiatives, alliances, coalitions, or partnerships.

Some examples of TSs in the non-profit sector include:

+ Intersectoral health collaboration — for example, substance abuse prevention projects involving police, educators, and service providers
+ Environmental collaboration processes — for example, the US Forestry Service excels at building TSs for more effective land and forest management
+ Community economic revitalization processes (see Chapter 10)
+ Partnerships for delivering human services, including services for youth and seniors
+ Advocacy coalitions — for example, groups advocating for anti-smoking bylaws
+ Operational partnerships (sharing space, expertise, etc.) — for example, two or more non-profit organizations pooling their resources to purchase shared services such as human resources management

Examples of TSs in the private sector

Typically, TSs in the private sector are joint ventures between firms to accomplish one or more of the following aims:

+ Gain a foothold in the international marketplace
+ Foster innovation in the industry by conducting joint research and development (R&D)
+ Establish a unique position in the market
+ Boost market presence
+ Provide added value to customers
+ Expand each organization's customer base
+ Access knowledge and expertise beyond company borders
+ Increase sales and profitability
+ Reduce overhead by sharing costs or outsourcing
+ Enhance research and development capability
+ Strengthen reputation in the industry as a result of association
+ Extend product or service offerings
+ Speed entry into a particular market
+ Establish advantageous purchaser/supplier relationships
+ Set up distribution networks

Some of the private sector structural tools used to formalize a TS include hollow partnerships, consortia, cross-licensing agreements, internal networks, compact agencies, and virtual partnerships.[6]

Examples of private/public TSs

Often a TS offers a bridge between the private and public sector. For example:

- Social marketing campaigns can strengthen a company's reputation in the industry as a result of association with a non-profit, while at the same time bringing revenue and volunteers to the non-profit organization.
- Public policy task forces can involve both corporations and government to resolve policy disputes, develop consensus on new policy directions, and solve shortages of skilled labor.
- Community economic development can help both private and non-profit sectors cope with economic decline, while revitalizing a community.
- Business and university research consortia can result in an exchange of expertise: the private company can save money on R&D, and the university can access funding from the private sector.
- Multilateral collaboration (between nations, non-government organizations, multinational corporations) can achieve global management of resources and deal with trade issues.

What does the literature tell us about TSs?

Until now there has been little documentation about the development of this organizational form. Handbooks and primers on creating TSs in the private sector do exist, but they tend to focus on the details that can be translated into a legal document at the end of the day. In material targeted at the non-profit sector, the description of how to develop the organization often gets mixed up with the work objectives. At best, authors provide nine or ten principles to consider when creating and maintaining a TS.

Usually these principles include:

- Develop mutual trust
- Develop shared goals and sense of purpose
- Work with others
- Develop appropriate leadership
- Find common ground
- Tolerate difference
- Encourage participation
- Be flexible
- Have a sense of humor
- Start small and get some early wins

These are sound principles, but they do not convey the practical details involved in creating a complex organization.

When community developers pioneered the early TSs, it seemed to outsiders that they did so easily and naturally. The developers appeared to operate on an intuitive level and had the personalities and social skills that made it easy to apply the above principles. As one of those early developers, I can attest to the amount of work involved, the skills that I had to develop, the knowledge bases that I had to master, and the copious amounts of blood, sweat, and tears that I shed as I traversed the uncharted waters of TS formation.

Professionals facilitating and supporting TSs today — academics, nurses, and dieticians — often have a high degree of technical training, but they too may have minimal experience or training in leadership and group development. They need these principles turned into solid steps for action, which is what I hope this book will provide.

How does a TS work in practice?

The prototype for the trans-organizational system is the symphony orchestra. Each of the musicians in an orchestra is a specialist, but they all have to work together to perform a piece of music. Every person's instrument has its own unique voice and role. Each is significant. Each contributes. The result would not be the same if even one was absent. Yet when they all play together, the result can be cacophony or music. It all depends on the score and the conductor. The conductor must ensure that the musicians understand all the parts and how they fit together to make a coherent whole. While each musician is allowed space to express himself or herself, the whole thing — hopefully —comes across as a single beautiful composition. Giving space to others to take their turn in the spotlight, and taking space yourself to make a contribution to enhance the end product, is also critical to making beautiful music and a great organization.

In a TS, each of the organizations is a specialist, like individual musicians. The TS coordinator or manager works like a symphony conductor. The coordinator's task is to help the group develop a common vision and agreement on the task at hand and then coordinate all the specialists/members to undertake their piece of the vision and strategic plan. All members must deeply understand all the parts of the TS and must recognize what they need in order to create a harmony among them that will allow them to move forward to their common desired future.

Benefits of TSs

There are numerous benefits to a trans-organizational system, some of which have been mentioned in passing earlier. These include the following advantages:

- A TS can be used to organize or rationalize a multi-organizational human service delivery system or supply chain.

- A TS can encourage increased flexibility and creativity for addressing changes in the environment or new issues. Multilevel responses built upon alternative perspectives are more likely to occur. The broad spectrum of expertise, experience, and perspective among TS members leads to the potential for novel ways of thinking, new ideas, and innovative solutions. The TS form provides opportunity for creativity and ingenuity.

- A TS can expand resources available to deal with problem sets and challenges. The funding and knowledge of the sector or community are maximized. There is no need to "reinvent the wheel" because the "right hand" comes to know what the "left hand" is doing.

- TS participants' perceived legitimacy to act upon the problem or problem set increases. With many organizational members, the TS's span of influence can expand to achieve many desired outcomes. For example, a TS of senior citizens' groups may not only achieve desired health outcomes, but may also find that other issues affecting seniors, such as crime prevention, get addressed as well.

- Funders love to see a plan that is endorsed by many partners. Because a consensus is developed within the TS, and its collective strategic plan involves most of the interested stakeholders, the opportunity for opposition is reduced. Funders and political leaders are more likely to jump on the bandwagon, as they are exposing themselves to less risk of upsetting a major player in the sector/community, and the plan and projects will more likely succeed if everyone is onboard from the beginning.

- TS participants find themselves part of something larger than just their own organization. They are part of a sector or a community with expanded social networks and access to resources. The whole becomes greater than the sum of its parts.

- A TS often becomes the meeting place where deals and opportunities happen This benefit is rarely the reason for forming a TS, as networking itself is not considered a solution to a problem but a means to finding a solution. However, relationships formed within a TS are highly valued. For instance, individual agency partners often find that they can do a reality check on new ideas for their own agency programming by presenting them to TS members for feedback before they go to pilot testing. TSs are the place to meet with peers and colleagues and catch up on the latest sector or community news. These meetings can also resolve conflicts before they escalate due to lack of communication or lack of opportunity to clarify rumors or misunderstandings.

+ When funders and government program officers are included as part of the TS, they are exposed to the day-to-day realities of their transfer agencies and the ultimate end users of their programs. Government or funder decision-making becomes more grounded in reality. Policy development takes on local roots.

+ Because of their nonhierarchical structure, TSs offer an increased opportunity for participants to experience *personal gratification* by having an impact on seemingly insoluble problems or through the joy of being able to operate in a democratic organization.

Challenges of TSs

On the other hand, trans-organizational systems face a great many challenges. These include the following issues:

+ It is often difficult to bridge the diverging aims, interests, and cultures of member organizations. It is not easy to overcome silos of thinking and develop a common agenda.

+ People must make a significant time commitment to build the capacity of the new group. All parties must participate in the discussion and decision making or nothing will happen. Information must be shared, and systems must be developed to allow this to happen.

+ Power and status differences among partners can lead to a mistrustful atmosphere, which may occur from day one or arise at other times in the group process.

+ Differences in members' resources and capabilities can lead to relative dominance or passivity instead of equal participation. There may also be a tendency to rely on the facilitator/coordinator to do everything.

+ It is difficult to balance the need for a careful process to create an effective TS with the urgency to achieve the task for which the organizations are partnering. The hidden personal agendas of participants can derail the process, or personal expectations may exceed group goals.

+ Ingrained cultural assumptions regarding gender differences can result in an imbalance in "airtime" (speaking time) during discussions and decision making and in expectations as to who should actually carry out the tasks in the strategic plan. This is true of any organization, but is exacerbated in TSs because of their political nature and the performance anxiety that may come with large group dynamics.

- There are many communication issues, including those that exist with established relationships. However, new groups and relationships are particularly prone to problems, such as misunderstandings, when each organization already has its own way of communicating. There is a need to develop a common language for communication.
- There is often a lack of resources for the extra capacity building required, partly because funders are reluctant to invest in capacity building when the limits are unclear.
- Turnover of individual participants during the life of the TS leads to poor group process. Since participants carry the organizational memory, when they leave there are big holes that need to be addressed while bringing newcomers up to speed.

In the book *Organization of the Future*, editors Frances Hesselbein, Marshall Goldsmith, and Richard Beckard cite statistics from an Anderson Consulting survey which indicate that over 85 percent of the top executives in telecommunication industries, and over 95 percent of those in health care, believe that alliances are essential to their future. However, most of these same executives expect their alliances will fail to deliver on the promised value. In fact, the vast majority of alliances do fail and are soon dissolved.

But the challenges of forming successful alliances can be met if you address one of the key issues. The primary difference between an organization and trans-organizational system is how power is handled. Because a TS is based on the need for members to share responsibility for the problem or problem set, and therefore to share power, the organization's architecture itself must be organized to take this power-sharing characteristic into account. A TS cannot centralize power to a few decision makers at the top of a hierarchy and expect member organizations to comply. Compliance is voluntary for members, so their participation in decision making is critical. In Chapter 4, I will address the issue of power in detail. Power is an important lens through which to perceive the issues and conflicts that strain the TS form of organization.

In the rest of this book I present the concepts and tools you need to build the trust and create the value for working together collaboratively.

CHAPTER 3

A Development Framework for Trans-Organizational Systems

Where do you find common ground? At the point of challenge!

Jesse Jackson

In 1984, Thomas Cummings wrote a seminal article entitled "Trans-organizational Development." This article has influenced my work on TSs more than any other research except the Open Systems theory developed by Eric Trist and the Emerys. I have adapted the concepts Cummings articulated into the TS development framework in Figure 3.1.

3.1: *Development Framework for a TS*

Phase 1

Determining the need for a TS and exploring the problem set

What intractable problems are surfacing in our environment that we cannot resolve by ourselves?

↓

Phase 2

Motivation to collaborate

We decide to act in concert with others because of the perceived benefits of collaborative action.

↓

Phase 3

Member identification and selection

Who cares about the problem and is willing to join our process?

↓

| **Phase 4** |
| **Collaborative planning** |
| Should a TS be created? If so, what are its vision and action strategies? |

↓

| **Phase 5** |
| **Building an organization** |
| How do we organize the vision and action into structure, leadership, communication, policies, and procedures? |

↓

| **Phase 6** |
| **Evaluation** |
| How is the TS performing in terms of performance outcomes, quality of interaction, and member satisfaction? |

Adapted from Thomas G. Cummings, "Trans-organizational Development." *Research in Organizational Behaviour,* Vol. 6 (1984), pp. 367-422.

Phase 1: Determining the Need for a TS and Exploring the Problem Set

Problems that call for a TS are often complex or ill-defined. Obviously, a problem that is easily solved by one organization does not need a multi-organization response. It would be a waste of time, energy, and resources to enter into a complex organization-building process when it is not necessary.

Phase 1

Determining the need for a TS and exploring the problem set

What intractable problems are surfacing in our environment that we cannot resolve by ourselves?

A TS may be required when several stakeholders have a vested interest in the problems and are willing to work together developing solutions. A TS is even more appropriate if there is a history of incremental or sporadic efforts to deal with the problem set that have not produced satisfactory solutions and the problem seems to be unsolvable or exasperatingly persistent.

Environmental scanning

Environmental scanning is a process of learning about the problem. It is also the name of a tool used to assist in the learning process. In the 21st century, all information workers need to monitor the environment and explore its complexity every day because of the rapid course of events. It is a critical skill in an active adaptation process (i.e., for creating responses to events) both on an individual and an organizational basis. You look at what is happening in the external environment and explore how it relates to your work and the problems or problem set you are dealing with.

Environmental scanning is now considered one of the most important functions of a senior manager in a work organization. It is also critical for generating and assessing courses of action to deal with complex problems and their environments. Paying attention to events, patterns of events, and societal and economic drivers over time provides a knowledge base for decision making. Continuous environmental scanning can also help identify opportunities for capitalizing and leveraging. For example, non-profit organizations can keep track of new trends in funding opportunities. If funders want to prioritize certain neighbourhoods or groups, you might hear about it by attending community meetings and by monitoring political speeches and scuttlebutt. Private business operators do this by keeping informed of their industry and by watching what their competitors are doing.

When I am assessing the possibility of establishing a new TS to address a problem, I open two files, a paper file and an electronic one. In the files I keep newspaper clippings, magazine articles, references, and key contact information. By opening a file, I am telling myself that I am committed to an exploration phase. I acknowledge the problem as one I am expending energy on and, therefore, as one that I might want to address at some point. The file represents, symbolically and physically, the collection of data that I will use to connect the dots into analysis and to identify possible solutions and possible partners. For instance, since I work in the non-profit sector, funding announcements or changes to client populations, such as the imminent arrival of a new refugee group, could be pertinent to problems that concern me. In the private sector, critical data could emerge around marketing, competition, economic trends, or any aspect of doing business in the world today.

This phase can take anywhere from five minutes to a lifetime. Is it a developmental phase? I believe so. If a problem is not identified, if people don't say to themselves and others that they need to solve it, nothing will happen. In the management literature on alliances, academics emphasize the need for a champion or change agent to develop a successful alliance. In the non-profit sector we are more reluctant to emphasize the need for individuals to provide leadership, but in my experience there is a similar need for a champion. Sometimes the champion must convene only the first meeting before the process takes on a life of its own, but even so, someone has to step up and begin the process or it does not begin.

Environmental scanning tools can be as simple as a SWOT exercise (which evaluates strengths, weaknesses, opportunities, and threats) or as complicated as activating a newsbot to monitor Internet traffic and exposure on a trend or topic.

Scenario planning

I use the data I collect to do scenario planning, another tool that explores further the complexity of the problem set. In scenario planning the TS initiator connects the dots (pieces of data) gleaned from the external environment and projects the implications of these dots on the system, whether it is an organization, sector, or community.

One simple but effective scenario-planning exercise is derived from the open systems theory tool of "search conference." With the data you have assembled from scanning the environment and opening a file, brainstorm seven to ten points that describe the future you most desire for the problem/problem set you are examining. This is your wish list in a perfect world. Then on a separate sheet of paper brainstorm seven to ten points that describe the most probable future. You can also develop a worst-case scenario to broaden your thinking, but much of it will probably be captured in the most probable future scenario.[1]

Orientation outside of one's own organization

At some point early in the process of issue exploration, you may recognize that your own organization does not have the capacity to solve the problem by itself. Whether due to the size and the complexity of the problem or to your own lack of resources, you understand that you cannot act alone.

Before I became involved in my first large-scale TS, that point of awareness came as I sat in a meeting of the City of York's land use committee in 1993. I was a city councilor for a small, aging suburb with a population of approximately 150,000. The problem set included a declining industrial tax base, the closing of shops on our main streets, ever-increasing social needs as we were an area receiving many immigrants, a major global recession, and a sky-high unemployment rate (30 percent). I was elected to a reform council a year after a major development scandal sent two council members to jail and left the entire community with a bad reputation.

Although the committee was dealing with urban planning issues, the conversation that day whirled around the need to attract investment, create jobs for our residents, and bring in tax revenue to provide needed social services. In the discussion of how to do it, I stated that this was not a problem we at city hall could solve alone; we needed the collaboration of all levels of government, our neighborhood associations, social agencies, and large and small businesses to develop a common vision and plan. I'm sure my comments took less than two minutes. Everyone agreed and said, "If you can do it, we'll support you." The Community Economic Development Committee for the City of York was born soon after, and I began learning about trans-organzational systems.

On the path to TS formation, someone always has to make the move to look outside their home organization for help with a complex problem. When this happens, organizational energy shifts focus and everything starts to look different.

Phase 2: Motivation to Collaborate

Whoever initiates the process does so because he or she is motivated to act. What are those motivators? They could be the benefits listed in Chapter 2, but often the key motivator is that there is a great likelihood of success if you move ahead and enroll others in the process. You can determine the likelihood of success through a brief analysis. The questions in the sidebar "A Simple Feasibility Assessment Tool" are a good starting point.

Phase 2
Motivation to collaborate
We decide to act in concert with others because of the perceived benefits of collaborative action.

A Simple Feasibility Assessment Tool

By working through the following questions you undertake a simple feasibility study. You will identify potential partners and their possible motivation for working with you on the problem set. The questions also lead you to identify likely strategies to address the problem and determine whether your potential partners might add value to the possible and probable solutions. The questions also help to clarify what potential impact creating a TS might have on your home organization.

- Are other individuals and organizations likely to be concerned about this problem too?
- Would they be willing to commit time and resources to the work involved on a long-term basis? What assets and capabilities might be exchanged in a partnership? What might our organization provide and expect to receive?
- Are there opportunities for solutions to be found and/or developed? For instance, are there sources of funding we could access?
- What kind of work would the group undertake? (In the non-profit sector, think beyond broad descriptors like revitalization and community development. Is it more likely to be advocacy, education and awareness, social marketing, or ☛

programming? In the private sector, is the solution likely to be a marketing- or a supplier-focused TS?)
- What kind of commitment would my core group and I need to make to get a TS up and running?
- How would this process help our organization to:
  - Serve our clients/customers?
  - Reach our strategic goals?
  - Achieve desired results?
- What risks might this alliance involve? What risks to each other's reputation? What financial risks?
- What other benefits might this partnership bring to our organization, to the community, to the industry?
- Given this preliminary assessment, is there a strong potential for a partnership that will further our organization's mission and serve our constituency better? ∎

If the assessment does not seem to bear out a substantive case for partnership, ask what you can do to improve conditions for a future partnership or to undertake a project in-house to explore the problem.

Personal assessment

On a personal level, I always find this a period of intense self-examination. It means I have to take a big personal risk and put myself, my values, and my beliefs out there for public consumption. I have to say "I don't know" more times than I can count in response to questions about what we are going to do. I have to build trust with people who don't trust easily anymore, and I have to be energetic, positive, and enthusiastic a good part of the time.

I undertake a personal feasibility assessment as well, asking myself questions like: What are my motives in doing this? Are there benefits for me? What are the risks?

I go through a lot of gut-wrenching self-examination. I ask myself things like: Who am I to believe I can make a difference? Why doesn't anyone else see what I am seeing? Why don't they do it?

Much of the time I overcome the fears and take the risk. Why do I do it? Often because I know I can. I have done it in the past and replicated it over and over. And I do it because I can make large-scale systemic change happen, even though it is considered a difficult thing to accomplish. However, I am more discerning these days and do not enter processes without explicitly stating what I can or can't do. I have learned to define my limits up front and only commit to what is feasible so that I do not overextend myself. Not only is this good for my health, but it encourages others to do the same. If we find we don't have the energy or resources, we can develop strategies to overcome the obstacles rather than having unrealistic expectations of each other.

You never get very far alone!

In a multistakeholder process, things happen because others choose to collaborate. Although you make a contribution, it is always the *others* who are the raison d'être of the process. Key people emerge who are more than willing to share the role of leadership, share ideas, provide feedback, share the workload, and encourage everyone to move forward to the next step.

Even when I was in an overt leadership role, there were always people behind the scenes who mobilized staff or monetary resources and did the key coordination work of organizing meetings and taking minutes. This is as much leadership as chairing a meeting. Without that work, nothing can happen. In the case of York's economic development committee, it was the director of economic development who bought into the process immediately and was as responsible for its success as I was. In another TS, started to integrate a newcomer group to my community, my executive assistant, who happened to have the same ethnic background as the newcomer group, was the key player in making it happen. Your colleagues are your partners. Without them the larger partnership process will not unfold.

When I have acted in a coordination role, there were always key partners who shouldered more of the responsibility. They happened to value collaboration too. I was blessed to have connected with them. We need colleagues who can affirm the value of a process when resistance or other challenges creep up. Issues and conflict will inevitably emerge in a TS, so find your support system and cherish the people in it.

Phase 3: Member Identification and Selection

In his 1984 article, Thomas Cummings identified member selection as the first stage of trans-organizational development. People sometimes gloss over it by saying whoever attends an initial organizing meeting is meant to be the membership. However, a more purposeful approach to membership identification reaps benefits in the long term. Cummings wrote, "Identifying stakeholders not only involves

Phase 3
Member identification and selection
Who cares about the problem and is willing to join our process?

judgments about resources and problem interests, but political assessments as well. Failure to identify and possibly include powerful stakeholders can weaken the TS's legitimacy and problem solving capability."[2] As I pointed out in Chapter 2, the knowledge resources of a TS are not individuals, but the specialist organizations. If some organizations are not part of your TS, you will not be able to draw on their knowledge.

Three ways of incorporating knowledge resources into a trans-organizational system

Knowledge resources are found within potential member organizations. The purpose of collaborating and forming a TS is to access and incorporate that organizational knowledge into a strategy to deal with the identified problem or issue. There are many ways to identify possible members for a TS and invite them to join, but most fall within the following three categories:

Expanding Network Model: In this membership selection process you begin with a small core group of organizations. As you learn more about the problem and its environment, you expand and recruit organizations and resources. These resources can be specific experts and leaders in relevant fields who are integrated into the TS or who are invited to participate on a time-limited basis when appropriate.

Stakeholder Analysis Model: In this process you identify your TS participants at the beginning of TS formation. You can use any of the following approaches to select participants:

+ Positional approach — Invite key staff in organizations that are connected to the problem and have a stake in the problem.
+ Reputation approach — Ask the community to suggest people through an interview or formal electoral process.
+ Social participation approach — Identify stakeholders based on their previous and current participation in efforts to solve the problem.
+ Opinion leadership method — Identify stakeholders on the basis of their leverage or influence in relation to the TS task.
+ Demographic method — Select participants on the basis of demographic characteristics that can affect the problem.
+ Referent group —A core group of organizations maps out the wider environment and identifies stakeholders.

Self Selection: This is the most common method. An issue champion calls a meeting of concerned persons and organizations. Whoever shows up and volunteers for a task becomes the new organization.

I strongly echo Thomas Cummings' opinion that you are doomed to failure if you do not include stakeholders who have the power to implement the TS recommendations. They may sabotage the process from the outset because they were not included.

At the same time, choosing the wrong partners or including participants who do not want the process to succeed is another recipe for failure. I once was hired to lead a TS process with a primary objective, "community revitalization," that was covertly opposed by the TS members. They equated revitalization with gentrification, which would lead to higher rents for their housing. They participated in order to ensure the process went nowhere — and they succeeded.

This raises the accusation that many TSs are really veiled co-optation processes. They can be if the convener's intention is to co-opt community mobilization or opposition. However, in most cases involving policy issues and urban or rural development projects, getting a number of different perspectives around a table is the only way to move forward. Consensus needs to be negotiated amongst the competing interests before any government can adopt a course of action. Sometimes the investment of time and funding in a TS is the only way forward, the only way to build trust over the long term. You may be accused of co-optation, but if you are clear and open about the need for a community consensus, your honesty will go a long way toward quelling the criticism.

Assessing partners

Once you have identified your major stakeholders through a stakeholder analysis, you can develop a second assessment to use in the conversation discussing their potential participation in the TS. This assessment is to determine whether they will commit, and fulfill their commitment, to participate in TS meetings and activities. If they cannot commit to attending meetings, consider building political goodwill by keeping them in the loop and sending them minutes of TS meetings. Often when potential participants see that real work is being accomplished, they will come into the process.

When you are assessing partners for a large TS, you (and they) may want to consider the following criteria:

+ Is there a clear match between their mission and the TS's focus?
+ Do they have good leadership and a membership/constituency with interest in addressing the problem?
+ Would they value an opportunity to have a voice in the decision making?
+ Would they be able to meet reasonable expectations of membership (i.e., share the workload, attend meetings, etc.)?
+ How do their organizational interests affect the TS's riskiness and viability?

+ Whose support or lack of it might significantly influence the success of the process?

When you are assessing partners for a small partnership, you might consider the following criteria:

+ What is their potential impact? Is there real value you can gain from a partnership that can't be achieved in another manner?
+ Do you share enough common values to provide a base on which to work together?
+ Is the environment conducive to partnering? Are funders supportive?
+ Are the potential partner's goals consistent with yours? Does the vision and value proposition of the TS support the organization of origin's strategic focus?[3]

When the TS is going to be a joint venture with only one partner, you might find the worksheet in Figure 3.2 helpful. It is designed to assess a number of potential partners when the user has predetermined the criteria he or she is looking for in a partner. For example, say your agency is looking for human resource expertise. You are talking to several other agencies as potential partners. Your predetermined selection criteria include:

+ That the service be available on an as-needed basis
+ That the service provider be familiar with the non-profit sector
+ That the fee for service be lower than that charged by private sector providers

You give each potential partner a score based on how closely it matches these requirements. The score for the criteria leads to the ranking in the last column, or the ranking can be tied to the number of criteria met. It may be that when you talk to potential partners, you discover that they have different ideas about how to cooperate and propose arrangements that you had not previously considered. Those proposals would be included in the Specific Arrangements column and could add points to the final ranking.

3.2 *Partnership Worksheet*

Benefits Sought	Potential Partner	Selection Criteria Met	Specific Arrangements	Rank
1	Resume screening for hiring processes and help with performance reviews	Y Agency	All	Y agency does not want to formalize the relationship through billing and invoices but trade the HR services for value equivalent services

A member's role

During the process of recruiting representatives from selected organizations as TS members, and in the initial organizing meetings of the TS, it is wise to negotiate and clarify what members' role will be vis-à-vis their organization of origin and their constituency, if they represent one. You can use the following questions to structure this discussion about power. Once TS members have agreed to a description of the members' role and to a process for making changes, these decisions can be recorded in the TS's terms of reference or a membership policy. This policy may need to be vetted by the senior staff of the organizations of origin if they are not sitting at the TS table.

Collectively, a TS may choose to empower everyone at the table with decision-making powers except when addressing the resources of the originating organizations. An originating organization may choose to outline in its policy the parameters of decision making for its representative or the expectations it has for representatives' reporting back. Reporting functions can range from sharing minutes of meetings to a formal requirement for meetings or annual reports.

- What is the role of representatives?
- Do they represent the view of a constituency?
- Do they have the authority to take binding action on behalf of their organization/constituency in TS decision making? If not, how will they secure approval for TS decisions?
- How will they report back to their organization of origin and their constituency?
- Can alternates serve in a representative's place?

Some writers exploring collaborative processes are now stressing the personal attributes of the members of a collaboration. They recommend choosing members with highly developed communication skills and a history of working collaboratively. I believe that healthy communication depends on a transparent and shared power structure. No matter how skilled people are in expressing their needs, they will not risk honest and open communication if it is unsafe to do so. I also find it elitist to demand skill sets that are not yet defined and only taught in some school systems. I would rather model appropriate behavior — such as owning my emotions, asking for what I need, and being comfortable with conflict (see Chapter 9) — than limit membership to people with the skills. It is invariably academically trained people who lack these skills, as they are products of a Western culture that values rationality above natural human expression.

Phase 4

Collaborative planning

Should a TS be created? If so, what are its vision and action strategies?

Phase 4: Collaborative Planning

Until members agree to a common vision, TSs are rudderless and directionless. The common vision acts like a route outlined on a road map, informing all who participate where the process will try to go. In this visioning and strategic planning phase you will develop the following:

+ Member commitment
+ Sense of mission
+ Shared values with which to work together
+ Collective vision
+ Goals that can be translated into action and be measured

This is the major trust-building and direction-setting phase in building a TS.

The first step in developing a vision and strategy is to limit the scope of the problem. If you haven't done it earlier, this is the phase in which TS members will agree on the extent of their collaboration. It is important that all parties know how much and what kind of effort they are committing to up front, since differing expectations can derail the proceedings. If you don't place boundaries around the problem, resources cannot be mobilized effectively and at a target. Endless, interconnected problems are the Achilles heel of TSs, particularly non-profit organizations. Effective facilitation and large system interventions can help with the task of setting these boundaries.

Organization development theorists have identified a process they call an *intervention*. An intervention changes a group dynamic; a conscious intervention is usually performed to improve the group dynamic. A *group dynamic* is best described as a characteristic of how the group is functioning. Each group is formed by the sum total of the individuals, their personalities, and the interactions between them. The group dynamic changes and grows through the process of working and sharing together.

Large system interventions are processes used by organization development consultants who are trying to get the whole system learning and making decisions at the same time. The objective is to have all the expertise and information pertaining to the system and its focus in the same room, able to make decisions in real time by exposing all the parts of an organizational system to the big picture. This enables people to make better decisions, incorporating not only their area of expertise, but also an understanding of how all the parts influence the whole.

Figure 3.3 identifies and assesses a number of large system intervention tools used by trained facilitators and organizational development consultants to help build trust among a diverse group and develop a common vision and implementation plan. They are particularly useful in the formation of a TS that has more than nine members. Group specialists have determined that nine is the number that changes group dynamics from those of a small group to a large group. Further information on each methodology can be found in the bibliography.

3.3: *Large System Intervention Tools*

Name of Process Tool	Description
Appreciative Inquiry	Appreciative Inquiry is currently popular. At its core is a process of reframing issues and problems positively when developing vision and strategic plans. AI process includes: 1. Definition: Frame the problem positively. 2. Discovery: Identify what works; connect to positive moments. 3. Dream: Create shared mages of a preferred future. 4. Design: Innovate and improvise ways to create that future. 5. Deliver: Implement the preferred future.
Search Conference	This is the most theoretically grounded intervention. SC is a two-and-a-half-day strategic or policy planning tool involving environmental scanning, system scanning, and strategy development in a democratic structure. It is the best tool for adapting to a turbulent environment and deals openly with conflict with a rationalization of conflict process.
Future Search	This is a popularized quasi-Search Conference methodology and search tool that was well-known and popular a few years ago. It modifies the traditional Search Conference with mind mapping and value identification exercises.

Name of Process Tool	Description
Institute of Cultural Affairs	ICA's strategic planning process is usually a three-part process involving a collective vision, identification of obstacles to that vision, and a strategy to deal with obstacles. Through the International Association of Facilitators, ICA has a worldwide organizational structure to support and promote the methodology.
Open Space	This is the most popular large system intervention at present. An Open Space leader sets ground rules for free-form discussions to take place. Participants identify topics, and gatherings form around posted topics in the village marketplace. These gatherings move into discussion space and participants self-organize to explore the topics. Many great ideas can be generated, but the methodology needs sufficient time and a trained facilitator to move the groups into idea selection and prioritization. This is also a good tool for bringing covert conflict into the open and allowing participants to work it out.
Preferred Futuring	This is an easy process for facilitators to learn and apply. It uses exercises similar to those in Search Conference and Future Search, including value identification and historical scans. The facilitator does not need to have a lot of theoretical understanding. It is flexible and adaptable to fit in available time frames. It brings the values of participants to the surface and encourages effective communication and trust building.

Phase 5: Building an Organization

Many TSs are stymied by this phase, in which members need to decide how to implement the vision and strategy developed in Phase 4 to address the problem. TSs are often built without members ever considering what they need to do to survive and carry out the agreed-to strategy. Instead of addressing that question and determining how much struc-

> **Phase 5**
> **Building an organization**
> How do we organize the vision and action into structure, leadership, communication, policies, and procedures?

ture is needed to ensure continuity and survival, members' energy is invested into implementing the strategy until conflict or lack of participation grabs everyone's attention or simply kills off the process. The group's architecture is neglected and the creation of the form (of the group) fails to follow the development of the function (the strategic response to the problem).

To ensure sustainability, the phase of organization building has to be consciously integrated into the work of building the TS.

How much structure is necessary?

The extent of structure necessary depends on four factors:

- The time period the strategy is designed to cover —The longer the time period, the more structure is needed to maintain the TS.
- How much system or organizational change is required by the strategy — Is there a need to have a broad coordination function apart from the projects or programs the strategy encompasses?
- Who has the resources to accomplish the change — Are the staff implementing the strategy hired by the TS or by the partners?
- How much management is necessary — Are there funds or staff that the TS has to manage?

Implementation is also the phase when collaboration between member organizations is particularly susceptible to breaking down. Barbara Gray, author of *Collaborating: Finding Common Ground for Multiparty Problems*, suggests this is due to the following reasons:

- Member organizations can change their priorities, policies, and staff.
- Proposed projects can be too difficult to bring to fruition.
- Conflict may arise — relations among stakeholders could deteriorate or they may already have a history of mistrust, animosity, and turf wars that erupts into conflict.

+ Cultural differences and expectations may create friction.
+ Organizational culture clashes may occur.
+ Turnover of members may affect group dynamics; newcomers need to acculturate into the existing group process.[4]

Three basic choices of organization design

In the 1930s, Kurt Lewin identified three basic forms of human organizations.[5]

+ Design Principle 1 (DP1): Authoritarian or hierarchal organizations
+ Design Principle 2 (DP2): Democratic organizations
+ Laissez-Faire: A form of organization that evolves haphazardly with little if any structural order

Each form takes a different approach to power and control and the way work is organized. In DP1 organizations, people are segmented into narrow job functions and are treated as replaceable parts (we know this as bureaucracy). The responsibility for control and coordination (the power to make decisions) lies with the supervisor or manager, at least one level above where the work is performed. This kind of structure is characteristically called a hierarchy.

In DP2 organizations, each person performs multiple functions — including social, business, and technical — using multiple skills. The individual is therefore more valuable to the organization and is not easily replaced. The responsibility for control and coordination is in the hands of the people doing the work. The power to make decisions is entrusted to the person closest to the work. This kind of structure is characteristically called democratic.

In laissez-faire organizations, there is no design principle and people operate without any parameters or direction to guide their work. Decisions are made covertly or aren't made at all. There is a general feeling of "do your own thing," without any thought for, or knowledge of, the needs of the broader system. Unfortunately, this system is often confused with a DP2 because people are thrown into "self-directed teams," even though they have no sense of direction or knowledge of the broader context to guide their work. People in a laissez-faire organization will frequently revert to DP1 behavior as a way to regain some control over the situation.

A TS, by its nature as an organization of organizations sharing power, can more easily operate as a DP2 organization than as a DP1 organization structured along hierarchical lines. Influenced by the changing metaphor for organization occurring throughout our society — from machine (hierarchy) to network or web (democracy) - many TS members are now entering and creating TS's with a DP2 mental model of structural relations. This is not always the case, however, and often TS members possess differing mental models.

It is critical, and often valuable, for you to try to make this conflict between mental models explicit at this stage and to get TS members to agree to adopt one or the other — preferably the DP2 model. You do not have to use the terminology of DP1, DP2 and the design principles, but it is advantageous to discuss expectations about who will have the power in the group. Will the boss be one person, a small group, or will leadership be shared?

The DP1 TS structure

Until the 1990s, most TSs, such as industry associations or even the United Nations, evolved as DP1 TS structures. The voices of individual organizations disappeared as power and control were assigned (through a constitution) to an executive committee or board of directors (in the case of the United Nations, to the Security Council). Participation in the organization's affairs was limited to those willing to be assimilated into a board of directors, who were then socialized to put the needs of the new organization first. Over time they began to feel little need to report back to or consult with their home organizations or constituencies

The representative power gleaned from a DP1 TS's member organizations is consolidated in the board of directors, which hires a CEO to manage association activities. Member participation takes the form of individuals sitting on committees and serving terms on the board of directors (see Figure 3.4). This representative form of governance does not assume or promote power sharing with the organizations of origin. We are familiar and comfortable with this model as it is the model for Western democratic government.

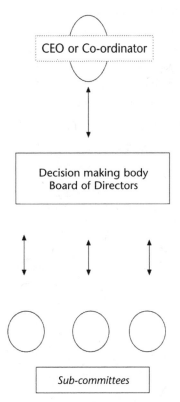

Laissez-faire TS structure

Unfortunately, TS members are usually so focused on responding to the turbulent environment and taking immediate action

3.4: DP1 TS

Horizontal boundaries remain, with approvals necessary up and down the hierarchy.

on their target problem that they fail to understand the need to develop an organizational structure. It is not until the group is mired in irresolvable conflict or fades away that members wonder what was missing. Without structure they acted like a herd of cats with no common direction or processes to take collective action

DP2 TS structure

Instead of replicating the stifling hierarchy of our home organizations or falling into the chaos of laissez-faire, a more effective approach is to create an adaptive and participative DP2 structure. This type of democratic structure arises from processes and policies developed through discussion and agreement, rather than from a DP1 organizational chart that appropriates power through role assignment up and down the hierarchy.

These days, many of the organizations that come together to form a TS may need or want to retain control over the long term in order to develop and shape the common vision and eventual programs and projects. As well, a TS developing an adaptive response to the turbulent environment may require frequent and rapid responses from the originating organizations and constituencies. They may need to share information quickly to facilitate rapid and innovative decision making, which requires a network of organizations rather than a top-down hierarchy (see Figure 3.5).

3.5: DP2 TS

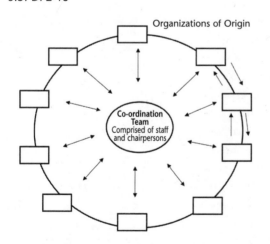

Organizations of Origin

Co-ordination Team
Comprised of staff and chairpersons

DP2 TS structures are almost always circular in design and resemble a network in structure.

It requires a conscious decision to create a DP2 structure, and the creation and maintenance of the democratic and participative forms of decision making, information sharing, and work sharing take a longer period of time and more resources than the establishment of a DP1 TS organization.

Chapters 5 to 9 provide in-depth information on the tools and processes needed to create this form of TS.

In my experience, few TSs ever reach Phase 5 and invest in developing the infrastructure necessary to sustain themselves. Minimal infrastructure can be fine when TSs have a limited focus such as advocacy, with no staff and fundraising activities, and will cease once the desired public policy initiative is implemented. But when governments download functions to TSs, including the funding of other organizations, it is vital to create the infrastructure to sustain a process for the longer term. You will note from the amount of time and space allocated to it later in the book that this phase is labor-intensive and much more complex than the creation of a traditional autonomous organization.

Phase 6: Evaluation

This phase is not necessarily the end of the process, but can signal renewal and moving thorough the development cycle again. All groups ebb and flow, achieving goals, then defining new directions. Some TSs end and permit something new to arise out of the ashes. The capacity built in member organizations and individuals always makes it possible for organizations to transform into new processes and strategic plans.

Phase 6
Evaluation
How is the TS performing in terms of performance outcomes, quality of interaction, and member satisfaction?

You can use "A Tool to Determine TS Effectiveness" (see next page) to evaluate the effectiveness of a TS as a group. This tool focuses on the functioning of the TS itself. It is an evaluation of the process by which the TS was developed and operates, not of the outcomes of the strategic plan and goals developed to deal with the problem or problem set.

Of course, both the TS group process and the strategy/goals/outcomes can be evaluated at the same time, but TS members may find it difficult to distinguish between the two. I find evaluators often mix together questions about the actions undertaken by the TS and the group process, and in such cases the feedback received is generally about the effectiveness of actions taken by the TS. It is best to do group process evaluations separately and more frequently than you evaluate outcomes attached to the vision and strategic plan. This will allow you to keep the process data distinct from the strategy and to respond to group process needs before small problems evolve into large ones.

A Tool to Determine TS Effectiveness

Phase 1: Determining the need for a TS and exploring the problem set
- Are we still relevant? Is the problem that catalyzed our coming together still motivating us to work together?
- Do members, clients, and people in the community still need us in the way that they used to?
- Are we gathering information from members, clients, and the community about their needs, wants, and preferences in relation to our focus?
- Is there ongoing data collection about the problem/problem set? To what extent is our TS scanning the horizon for new information and developments?
- Has a literature review been undertaken on the focus topic?

Phase 2: Motivation to collaborate
- Is a there still a perceived need for the TS in terms of areas of common interest and complementary capacity?
- Is there a clear focus for the TS? Does it still generate interest and commitment among member organizations?
- Are individuals emotionally connected to the purpose of the TS?
- Are we accessing and combining our collective knowledge resources? Can we access additional resources because of our collaboration?
- Are the organizations participating the same ones that were identified as the major stakeholders at the beginning of the process?
- Are participants willing to share some of their ideas, resources, influence, and power to fulfill the collective vision goal?
- Is the collaboration a strategic tool for each TS participant? For who?
- Are there cross-organizational interactions among other staff from member organizations?
- Who participates in the TS, senior or junior level staff? Does this impede decision making?
- Are there external forces providing an impetus or a mandate for cooperation?

Phase 3: Member identification and selection
- Are the TS participants developing common understanding of the problem focus?
- Are positive relations developing between the participants?
- Is there enough variety among members to have a comprehensive understanding of the issues being addressed and to facilitate a puzzle-learning approach?
- Are participants developing the necessary skills for collaborative action?
- Is there a participant not at the table who should be involved in the process?
- If so who? ☛

Phase 4: Collaborative planning

- Are all partners involved in planning and setting priorities for collaborative action?
- Has a neutral facilitator led the group through this phase?
- Has the process worked through its purpose or mission? Are our purposes and priorities clear to our members and external stakeholders?
- Has the TS developed a collective vision to respond to the problem set?
- Have differences in organizational priorities, goals, and tasks been addressed and resolved satisfactorily?
- Have all partners committed to the common goals and strategic plans?
- Does the strategic plan clearly show objectives, tasks, responsibilities, and target dates for review and completion?

Phase 5: Building an organization

- Does the TS frequently engage in trust-building processes?
- Are there governance structures in place that address decision and policy making?
- Are there staff members or assigned participants responsible for communication and work coordination?
- Is there a collective investment in the TS of time, personnel, materials, or facilities?
- Do TS participants feel comfortable to say what they think and feel in a way that promotes problem solving?
- When conflict arises, is the situation handled respectfully and effectively to everyone's satisfaction?
- Is a new organizational culture developing for the TS that includes, but is different from, the culture of the founding organizations? Culture is defined as a common language, shared organizational history, and shared beliefs and values.
- If a project fails, or things go less well than planned, do participants learn from it, and is their readiness to continue to try new things undiminished?
- Is there is a participatory decision-making system that is accountable, responsive, and inclusive?
- Are the roles, responsibilities, and expectations of partners clearly defined and understood by all other partners?
- Are issues and questions about power addressed openly and transparently?
- Are the lines of communication, roles, and expectations of participating organizations clear?
- Are processes that are common across organizations — such as referral protocols, service standards, data collection, and reporting mechanisms — standardized?
- Are there feedback loops to the organizations of origin and other stakeholders? ☞

Phase 6: Evaluation

- Are there processes for recognizing and celebrating collective achievements and/or individual contributions?
- Can the TS demonstrate or document the outcomes of its collective work?
- Are there resources available from either internal or external sources to continue the TS?
- Is there a clear need and commitment to continue the collaboration in the medium term?
- Do people regularly attend full TS meetings?
- Is there a way to review membership and bring in new members or remove old members?
- Has the TS developed a learning culture?
- Are there regular opportunities to reflect on how things are done and how they could be improved?
- Is there a mechanism for transferring knowledge from originating members to new members and from the TS to the community and stakeholders? ■

Power and Trans-Organizational Systems

Large numbers of large organizations, all acting independently in many diverse directions, produce unanticipated dissonant consequences in the overall societal environment, which mount as the common field becomes more densely occupied, especially when further limited by a finite resource base drawn on by all, the corporation can no longer act simply as an individual entity but must accept a certain surrender of sovereignty, much as the nation state.

H.V. Perlmutter and Eric Trist,
Paradigms for Societal Transition in Human Relations[1]

Gareth Morgan, in his groundbreaking book *Images of Organizations*, identified the various lenses or mental models that we can use when entering a new organization. Because of my political background, the first lens I often use is one that identifies and brings to the surface the organization's power dynamics. From my perspective, organizations are *the* stage where we enact the drama of human power relations. They are inherently political because they are human systems. It is even more critical to illuminate the power relations and dynamics in a TS form of organization, because often the group aspires to the DP2 model, but ends up operating as a DP1. In order to attain the equal power relations of DP2, the power structure and relationships must be much different from those in a traditional hierarchical organization. Members of a TS must consciously develop a democratic structure, which is reflected in the group's policy and decision-making processes. If they simply make decisions by default, or leave them to "the leaders" (acting in the traditional management role of a hierarchy), the TS structure will likely revert to DP1.

In *The Fifth Discipline*, Peter Senge pointed out that we all bring unconscious mental models into the organizations we join. We need to be aware that we bring along a mental model of a traditional hierarchical organization with us as we create a TS. Feminists call the mental model "internalized patriarchy." Many feminists have found that no matter how hard we try to build truly egalitarian organizations, we fail because we operate from the mental model of patriarchy, with its hierarchical power relations. Starhawk, the author of *Truth or Dare: Encounters with Power, Authority, and Mystery*, defines hierarchical power as power over and power under, rather than power *with*, which is the power relationship of a DP2 organization.

POWER implies possession of the ability to wield force, permissive authority, or substantial influence whereas
AUTHORITY implies the granting of power for a specific purpose within specified limits.

What is Power and Where Does it Come From?

For the purposes of this book, in the context of organizational power I will use the Merriam-Webster online dictionary definition of power as "the possession of control, authority, or influence over others." In other words, power is the right to govern or rule or determine the course of events.

You acquire the ability to wield force or exert authority from a source of power. When you have access to a power source, you have access to a form of power. We can explore the concept of power even further by exploring formal and informal sources of power.

Sources of formal power include:

+ Formal authority vested in positions and titles
+ Control of scarce resources
+ Control of structure, rules, and regulations
+ Control of decision-making processes
+ Control of knowledge and information or expertise
+ Control of boundaries
+ Control of technology

Sources of informal power include:

+ Ability to cope with uncertainty
+ Interpersonal alliances, networks, and control of informal organizations
+ Systemic power associated with class, ethnicity, and race
+ Symbolism and the management of meaning
+ Control of beliefs and social mores
+ Gender and the management of gender relations
+ Structural factors that define the stage of action (for example, Canada, as a neighbor to the US, has little power to choose a separate path from the US in foreign relations or drug control policies. The US doesn't

order Canada to choose a particular decision; it just threatens to delay border crossings in order to firm up its security. The US is bigger and richer. Canada is not as big or as rich. This is the structural factor and it is informal because it is not formalized by written agreement.)
- Personal power and confidence
- Charisma and/or the capacity to create fear in others
- An ability to communicate

Once you have access to a source of power, you have to be careful about when you use it or need it. The power you have access to may not apply in all areas of life or be useful in all situations or with all kinds of people. However, power is accessed all the time, in all kinds of situations, by many people. Everyone always has some power. There are no totally powerless people.

In a TS, different people access power at different times along the development journey. Before a formal organizational and decision-making structure is established, power can be assumed by those who take the following actions:

- Convene the process
- Select the participants
- Assume the role of host or initiate the process of inclusion for participants
- Present the problem set or issue
- Set meeting agendas
- Participate in discussions with an authentic voice (operating from their own interests and perspectives)
- Coordinate the meetings and activity between meetings
- Develop the process plan
- Make decisions outside of meetings and decide who can participate in backroom decision making

Many different sources of power can be used at the various junctures in TS formation. Be aware of them! Decisions are being made all the time. It may seem that no one cares during the early stages of the TS because nothing much is at stake. However, as time goes on, maybe because the TS gets positive attention from media or funders, those participants who are sensitive to power plays in day-to-day activities — or who are fearful that their interests may be affected when decisions are made covertly — will begin to express their distrust in the process. This distrust most often takes the form of not implementing the decisions and agreements adopted by the group, arguing about red herrings or inconsequential issues, or spending too much energy on ensuring the process followed is just right. With one TS I was involved in, a particular participant, after refusing to buy into a collective vision for action, stymied any further action by the group because of its lack of a collective vision.

This does not mean that you should not make decisions. If no one exercises the power to call people together so they can work to improve the situation, nothing will ever happen. The dilemma calls for transparency and honesty. When someone assumes the power at any of the choice points in the formation of a TS, that person must be explicit about what he or she is doing, with whom, and why. This is critical to building trust. Hidden agendas will only undermine the process.

If you are convening a process, you should use your power judiciously and openly until the group's power can be translated into formal authority vested in democratic decision-making processes and policies.

In her book *Negotiating at an Uneven Table*, Phyllis Beck-Kritek points out that our paradigm of power is based on the concept of dominant power. We do not acknowledge that there are other forms of power exercised by those without access to traditional dominant power sources. A democratic TS ideally should make room for those without dominant power sources. The trust-building tools and governance frameworks provided in this book can help integrate those participants who are ill at ease in meetings and in spaces where dominant power is the norm. As every person who was ever in a subordinate power position knows, there is great power in disengagement. For example, managers in traditional assembly-line factories know that they will face sabotage and/or high rates of defective product if they impose unwelcome controls over factory workers. Engagement is the objective in forming a TS, so you need to engage people consistently and enthusiastically or the whole process fails.

Power Games

Within a dominant power paradigm, power politics are traditionally played out constantly. Many people are totally unaware of the games that are played. One example, which I call "Jockeying for Position," is a traditional power game played in a meeting where people are coming together for the first time. In the game, players compete for airtime (talking space) in the meeting. Think of the time allocated for the meeting as a playing field. The objective of the game is to occupy as much of the field as possible, thereby preventing your opponents (i.e., everyone else in the meeting) from hearing other opinions or assigning much weight to them. You win the game if the group adopts your ideas and perceives you as the rightful leader of the group, based on your ability to influence. Those people who never share an opinion or voice anything are considered nonplayers on the sidelines.

Some people don't play the game on the same playing field. Those participants who have authority and power vested in some form of officialdom or extraordinary power in the process need not play Jockeying for Position, as their claim to leadership is publicly recognized by all. They have authority that came from winning an election or making powerful friends who owe them and have appointed them to a position of formal authority. I am speaking from my experience as a city councilor and activist/lobbyist, but the same dynamic can occur when a hospital with a highly paid CEO and multimillion-dollar budget engages with a community-based health TS, or when a level of government initiates a TS.

The strategy for the powerful and those with authority is to let the aspiring political players jockey for position. Then the person with authority swoops in right before the end of the meeting and present the facts from an insider's view, ensuring that the outcome he or she supports is accepted before anyone can ask embarrassing questions. Thus the meeting ends successfully for them. The players in the Jockeying for Position game may not know what hit them, but they all acquiesce (unconsciously) and vow to come back another day when the powerful one doesn't show up.

The moral of the story is that meeting participants who don't speak aren't in the political part of the meeting game. Often those who don't participate in the covert competition are women or members of ethnic groups who may be socialized to avoid direct confrontation and political conflict.

To avoid this dominant political dynamic from taking over, the TS leadership needs to integrate mechanisms that encourage participation from all members. Chapters 6 to 9 are filled with such tools.

It is hard work to confront those who skillfully use the rules of the power game and ask them to allow others a place and a voice. However, the reason we are going down this road in the first place is to share power and responsibility for outcomes. It is easier to structure the meeting with tools that facilitate open discussion than to overcome the politicking by your own interventions or backroom maneuvers.

Executive directors or coordinators often take the route of backroom planning and member massaging/manipulation between meetings. Covert activity that happens between meetings and behind the scenes breeds distrust in a group. It is also exhausting for those engaged in the manipulation and deception.

A Conceptual Framework of Power in Traditional Organizations

The first element of power in a TS is the design principle that is adopted, consciously or unconsciously, by the group. The design principles described in Chapter 3 explicitly address how power is exercised through control and coordination functions.

Using the DP1/DP2/laissez-faire conceptual framework, I began to understand that TSs often develop as laissez-faire organizations. The group develops without a conscious awareness of who is making decisions, and it often reverts to a DP1 organization with a small clique of decision makers behind the scenes.

My experience is that the adoption of a design principle must be made explicit. If it is not, members express their opinions and make decisions based on differing assumptions about, and mental models of, the underlying structure. Conflicts rooted in assumptions about design principles breed discussions that don't go anywhere — except to a laissez-faire structure and dysfunctional group process. If the TS has made a decision not to have open and democratic decision making about every issue (perhaps the TS is geographically dispersed or needs centralized decision making for some reason), you may decide to adopt a DP1 structure. The group can state that this is so and draw boundaries around the topics that will or won't be openly discussed. This will clarify a great deal and reduce tension considerably.

The discussion about which design principle to adopt is most likely to come up in Phase 5 of the development framework identified in Chapter 3. When you put the vision and strategic plan into operation, you also build the structural capacity for implementation through discussions and decision making. Starting off those discussions with a decision about power and design will smooth the way to the other processes. (If using the term "design principle" is too much jargon for your group, you can use the terms "democracy" (DP2), "hierarchy" (DP1), and "anarchy" (laissez-faire), which are familiar to most people.

Power in a TS

Because TSs are organizations of organizations, power relations can evolve quite differently than they do in traditional 0 or business organizations. The base of power comes from the organizations that choose to participate. Their participation and commitment is built one step at a time, and gradually they assign their power to implement the collective vision and strategy.

Power is also there for the taking, and just by broaching the possibility of bringing groups together to begin to discuss the idea of working together, you are exercising the power to seize the moment. Why do you get to exercise the power and not others? Sometimes it is simply because you choose to and they choose not to.

Once you or your organization seizes the moment and presents the idea of working together and moving ahead, power issues can appear at the following junctures.

Conceptualization stage

Before recruiting others to become involved, TS champions/steering committee members must determine the preliminary scope of problem solving and decision making for the TS. This generally takes place in the first three phases of development. Boundary setting for the problem set may even continue into the Phase 4, the visioning phase, if the problem set is complex and if TS members agree. The boundaries around the problem should be resolved by the end of Phase 4 or the vision and strategy will not be targeted effectively. If the problem has no boundaries, prospective members will sense a never-ending process with no focus.

By naming the problem that needs addressing, you are assuming the power to do so. This alone can shake up many people. Denial of the problem is one of the principal defense mechanisms in human systems. By naming a problem you stir up anxieties and the fear of change, and therefore people see you as having the power to disrupt the status quo.

Equalizing the playing field through language

It is unfortunate that as each discipline and profession becomes specialized, it develops jargon and language to facilitate speedier communication within the profession, which at the same time alienates those outside the profession. When specialists come together with volunteers or members of other professions, it is necessary to create a common language. Otherwise, the use of language becomes a barrier to listening, understanding, and working together and becomes a power differential.

The issue can be raised as soon as TS members start to meet. Defining terms and building a common lexicon should start as soon as possible. Otherwise the power to alienate and exclude will be at play in this stage.

Choosing partners

How are members going to be selected? How do you determine the legitimacy of stakeholders or potential TS members? Generally, people from Western countries believe they are entitled to participate when they will be affected by decisions. You can also determine if potential stakeholders have some power or influence over the problem set. Can they mobilize or organize people and resources? Do they have information or expertise, access to decision makers, or control over key institutions with a mandate that affect the problem set? (There is a discussion of various member selection processes in the Phase 3 section of Chapter 3.)

It is prudent to ensure that partners are engaged with the problem/problem set and are not just seeking side benefits such as access to decision makers. You need to establish a balance between the major sectors involved (government, nongovernmental organizations, business, academia, etc.), the needs of individual groups, and the common goals.

There is a great deal of power in determining who are to be the first members. It is the power to include or exclude. Later in the process (Phase 5), participants have to agree on who gets to choose new members by developing explicit criteria in the TS's terms of reference or membership policy.

Sheer numbers of interested or entitled partners can sometimes be overwhelming. In this case you must establish a process for selecting representatives or delegates. By engaging a broader constituency in choosing TS members, you share power more openly than you do when using a closed-door selection process. At this point, it is appropriate to work out time frames and mechanisms for reporting back to the representative constituencies.

Determining partner accountabilities

In a TS we need to create systems built on the assumption that everyone can be helped to assume a greater degree of accountability for managing their own work and for sharing in the "ownership" of the whole enterprise to which they are collectively committed. Enough trust and commitment needs to be generated that the work and knowledge is shared by the TS members.

The political trap with this issue is the "free rider." Many people will try to hitch a free ride and expend as little of their own time, energy, and money as possible. This behavior is illustrated by the popular saying "The way to get rich is to spend other people's money." If you find there are free riders in your TS, someone has to confront them and hold them accountable to the interests of the collective.

An asset-based development approach is now popular for broad-based community processes. In this approach, participants are selected based on the strengths and assets they can contribute to addressing the problem set, rather than by looking only at weaknesses and challenges to be addressed by professional service planners. Holding people accountable for their strengths and successes is much easier than focusing on what are deemed to be problems or failures.

Another accountability issue concerns how a member chosen to represent the interests of a particular sector is going to provide feedback to that sector about the decisions made by the new TS. Feedback processes can be as simple as sharing minutes or as complex as regular reporting or consultation meetings. With all of these accountability processes, you need to decide how far to formalize feedback loops.

The power of participants to make decisions

Are the partners sitting at the table able to make decisions on behalf of their organization? Can they contribute and buy into a visioning process? If they are not organizational decision makers, they must be able to secure commitment from their organization to any decisions made by the TS.

If frontline staff sent to join a TS process have never been involved in strategy development and are not empowered to make decisions on behalf of their agency, the result can be a stalemate in the TS. Each member organization needs to decide internally the amount of decision-making power that they can delegate to their TS representative.

First decision-making point

Are decisions going to be made by majority or by consensus? Generally, the champion or the driver of the process makes covert and overt decisions about naming the problem set or defining the issue and member selection. When a TS undertakes a visioning process, especially if outside consultants are used, the vision is developed through a consensus process (see the section on large system intervention methods in Chapter 3).

It is in Phase 5 — the operational phase — that decision making becomes problematic. Does the process convener continue to control decision making or is every decision put before the entire group and all member organizations? I have seen processes where no decisions are recorded in the minutes. I have also been involved in processes where the funder chose the decision-making process, but the group was never aware of that fact. There is often confusion about what consensus means, with participants asking if individuals can block the process and if unanimity is required to reach consensus.

At the beginning of the first meeting you also have to decide how decisions will be recorded, how the minutes will be distributed, who will control the agenda, and how items will be put on the agenda. Address these questions openly and you will begin to build trust among participants.

Reaching agreement on problem analysis, vision, and goal development

Using a trained facilitator and a large system intervention tool can create a level playing field for analyzing the problem and setting the vision. If there is no neutral facilitator, it is much easier for partners with a particular agenda and viewpoint to dominate the discussion. As this is a whole phase in TS development, this is a critical juncture at which to share power. If power is not shared here, the TS will remain a DP1 or laissez-faire organization.

Developing a shared vision through a process of participation is what motivates the members to implement the vision. If there is no power sharing, there is less motivation for members to work to implement the strategy designed to address the issue.

Ownership of the vision and implementation plan

The pay-for-say principle that dominates negotiations involving intergovernmental programs will often emerge in a TS process. Those with more resources may feel entitled to more input into decision making. However, for the long-term health of the TS, those who are able to contribute more financial resources to vision setting and implementation should respect the contributions of other partners. Each partner must identify and recognize the contributions of all the others as valuable and integral to the success of the whole process.

Committing financial or staffing resources to the plan can also begin a power struggle if richer partners are unwilling to subsidize poorer partners and recognize shared power in decision making.

If the vision and strategic plan extend over a broader domain than is under the TS members' span of control and influence, you may need to consult with other stakeholders who have an interest in the problem set in order to extend the buy-in. This may happen in the case of a community strategic plan where TS members represent many constituencies, but they decide to take the plan out to the community for further consultation in order to build good will. You may also need to consult with the constituencies of the organizations of origin, or let them vet the plan, in order to broaden the buy-in of agency staff. In the case of government partners, the TS might schedule private meetings for their input. You may be consulting with these people for support (political, financial, etc.), to head off criticism, or to allay their fear that you're making a power grab which may lead to them fighting you.

When I was a city councilor and in charge of land use planning, we called this "getting a kick at the can." Developers would put forward proposals to build houses or buildings, and it would be their job to present the plans to all the parties that might have an interest in them or be affected by them. After each encounter, the developers would massage the plans in some way to reflect the concern of the interested parties. There was a legal adjudication process at the end of all this consultation and massaging, and if the developers could show that they had met with everybody and tried to adjust the plans to meet their concerns, there was a good chance the plans would be approved.

When everybody gets a kick at the can, you are bound to alienate or upset someone, and when you make changes to alleviate that person's concerns, you may find yourself going back to square one to make sure all your TS members are okay with the modifications. In a nutshell, this is why it is so hard to make large-scale change happen.

Is everyone equal?

I often hear the refrain: "We are all equal here, aren't we?" When the question is posed, the group needs to explore exactly how members need to feel equal, and it needs to formalize the conclusion of that discussion in the TS's governance framework. Are all members equal in terms of power to define the problem? Maybe one member has defined the problem with a prior report or even a funding proposal. In this case, it is up to the other partners to make explicit their need to redefine the problem or the way it has been interpreted. If someone has already assumed the power to do something, it does not mean that others can't stop the process temporarily and negotiate a change.

The mechanism by which power is shared must be negotiated and can be revisited over the life of the TS. That mechanism is usually a decision-making process and an articulation of the roles and responsibilities of those involved in that decision-making process.

Some members may be happy to give up the power to be involved in every decision made if it means that critical decisions can be made in a timely manner. For this to happen, however, they will have to have enough trust in those they assign power to that they are content with the unequal power relationship. Alternatively, they could develop parameters and criteria for the times and situations when the assigned power can be used. If there is not enough trust, they will have to suggest another decision-making structure, one in which everyone has to be involved in every decision.

Those who don't get to the table at all are the most unequal. Often it is only the most vocal who are invited to the table and gain prized access to the decision-making arena. The voiceless remain outside and hold the least power. It is always good process to keep this fact in mind and find ways to involve those outside the process. Distribution of meeting minutes and reports, as well as formal outreach presentations, can help to address the power imbalance with those not included in the TS decision-making process.

Formal agreements

For some processes, such as a community revitalization, a strategic plan that is broadly distributed and promoted is enough to ensure that the plan will be implemented. However, once there is programming or firm projects underway, you may need a formal agreement to enshrine TS member contributions and commitments.

Power Politics Outside the TS

The desire for power or the ability to influence power brokers are among the principal drivers or motivations behind aligning one's organizational forces with others. Let's face it. If one organization had the power to solve a problem or control the outcomes of a course of action, there would be no need for it to cooperate with others. Power issues percolate up and around all the processes of a TS.

Power issues also emerge outside the boundary of a TS and intersect and intertwine with the internal dialogue and structure building of the TS. Because a TS is a wonderful tool to build community consensus, it is also a prime target for political operators to infiltrate and attempt to control and influence.

Even the most skillful facilitator is rarely able to bring a hidden political agenda to the surface, as an element of secrecy is necessary in political intrigue. There may be members who advocate for a position publicly but are maneuvering behind the scenes for something entirely different. Politicians can also be assessing the TS to use it for other purposes, such as political organizing and mobilizing (can be problematic), or as planks in their political platform (may be a good thing). Many citizens and organizations will be doing the same thing — using the credibility and legitimacy of the TS to support various positions and causes. This is not necessarily wrong, but you must be aware of the possibility that it is happening because the dynamics of the group will change due to the covert nature of the political activity.

Covert dynamics and hidden agendas are difficult to deal with in any situation, but the best way to deal with anything covert is to make it overt and put out it for discussion. If you can bring the politicking into the open, it will not have the same destructive impact on group process as it does if left to lurk on the margins. This may be frightening, as it is not easy for people to confront one another. However, confrontation can be done gently and positively. You do not have to accuse loudly and with anger to put something on the table. You can share your feelings and suspicions without making an accusation. Instead of using the word "you," own your feelings by saying "I feel ... " Describe the behavior that is making you suspicious (for example, maybe you know someone is withholding information), share your feelings about the activity (perhaps you fear that TS members will lose trust if one member is perceived to be profiting from something), and then ask for validation by asking whether others feel the same way or not. (Sometimes we are unconsciously triggered by previous events from our own life so that we suspect something is happening, even when it is not. Asking for confirmation or validation helps determine whether you are the only person who feels something or if others do too.) If people are receptive to your perceptions, them move to ask for the kind of behavioral changes you want (in this example, you could ask that if TS members get notice of new funding opportunities, they share them with the TS). The issue may not be resolved to your liking, but the important thing is that the issue is on the table and can be talked about, rather than lurking around in the shadows of the group, breeding suspicion and mistrust.

A Unique Form of TS: Government-Initiated TSs for Consultation

Governments often bring a range of interests around a single table to determine how to deal with a public policy interest. Such multistakeholder processes may be used on an ongoing basis in an advisory capacity. They can also be used at certain points in a policy-development process — for example, to develop a position paper for further public consultation.

I am proud to acknowledge that multistakeholder processes are prevalent in Canada's governance framework. They are seen as a more collaborative way to develop policy than the traditional adversarial approach in which special interest groups vie for the attention of policy makers. In a multistakeholder process, diverse interests are supposed to work together to find common ground. The convening government recognizes that it does not have all the answers, but needs to involve responsible citizens, interest groups, and other levels of government to help find better, more lasting solutions to community problems.

However noble the convening government's intent, these processes can drive participants mad because the scope of decision making is rarely clarified. Governments will frequently set up multistakeholder processes to get input into decision making or to mobilize support for implementing the final outcomes, whether policies or programs. However, they neglect to tell participating organizations what the power parameters are or who gets to make the decisions. Sherry Arnstein's "Eight Rungs on the Ladder of Citizen Participation" (Figure 4.1) demonstrates the degrees of autonomy of this form of TS.

4.1: *Ladder of Participation*

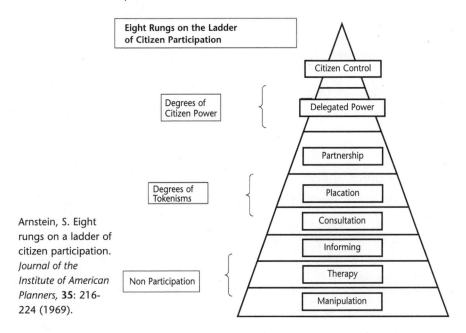

Eight Rungs on the Ladder of Citizen Participation

Degrees of Citizen Power

Degrees of Tokenisms

Non Participation

Citizen Control

Delegated Power

Partnership

Placation

Consultation

Informing

Therapy

Manipulation

Arnstein, S. Eight rungs on a ladder of citizen participation. *Journal of the Institute of American Planners*, **35**: 216-224 (1969).

Nonparticipation levels

At the bottom rung of the ladder, the "Manipulation" level of (non)participation, participants provide little input. They are merely invited to rubber stamp or validate the proposed course of action in order to head off criticism of those with power. This level can involve developing strategies for further compliance with what the experts perceive as the correct way to handle the issue.

At the second rung, "Therapy," participants are able to let off steam. I spent long hours as a municipal councilor hosting public meetings for this purpose. Although the city planners felt that holding public meetings showed they were progressive, the truth was that ordinary folks could do little to oppose a development plan. When they were finished venting they would be informed of their rights, and most would then give up and return home, nurturing their cynicism.

The third rung, "Informing," is the most prevalent form of participation used by all levels of government. It involves a one-way flow of information from the powerful to the powerless. E-government takes this to an extreme, as almost all government documents will be soon be online. Only a few people, and only those on the right side of the digital divide, are able to make sense of all that information.

Degrees of tokenism

At the "Consultation" rung there is two-way communication through either face-to-face public meetings or written submissions. Beware the convener who is only asking for input and not promising that the input will be incorporated into decision making. Consultation is often just window dressing to satisfy policy makers that there is support for the proposed course of action.

On the fifth rung, "Placation," a few hand-picked, "worthy" members of the public are placed on committees to represent the opposition. They might have some influence but are usually small in number, and those in power retain the right to make final decisions. It is vital that you are clear about the ground rules up front before taking part in such a process.

Degrees of citizen power

Participants on the "Partnership" rung agree on the responsibilities of power and structures. They help make the ground rules, which are only changed by mutual consent. A healthy TS would fall into this category.

On the seventh rung of "Delegated Power," participants have decision-making authority mandated from a higher authority and are legally able to make decisions. The community holds a majority of the seats on the committee and has power over a particular plan or program, usually as a result of negotiation.

On the top rung of "Citizen (or Worker) Control," workers, community members, or other participants are given full autonomy over an area and are put in charge of making policy and the managerial aspects of a decision. In Open Systems theory, this level of participation would result in a DP2 organization.

Working in this kind of TS

Government-initiated multistakeholder processes can occur at nearly every rung along this continuum. If you are involved in this form of TS, see if you can figure out where it fits on the Ladder of Participation. Except when you are on the lowest rungs — manipulation or therapy — you may find participation fruitful, depending on your own or your organization's needs. For example, although government distributes a great deal of information over the Internet these days, much useful information never sees the light of day. Participating on a government committee can give you insight into the decision-making apparatus of government and be helpful if you are awaiting decisions or seeking funding from government.

From an organizational dynamics point of view, if participants know what the purpose and process are, taking part in a multistakeholder process can be productive, though not as democratic as it might be. If you are a participant, ask questions so that you can determine the nature of the beast. If it turns out the process is purely for consultation purposes, there is no value in developing an operational architecture for the TS. A healthy decision-making process and enough trust to listen and build upon each other's contributions are about all you need to develop recommendations that will move into the bureaucracy and the political arena.

Kenneth Kernaghan, an expert in government and public administration, writing about government partnerships, observes that there are rarely equal power relations in government-initiated partnerships because it is risky and challenging for government to surrender its autonomy to partners outside government. He also describes a classification framework for government partnerships based upon the nature and extent of power exercised by each partner.[2]

- Consultative partnerships: Government solicits input from individuals, groups, and organizations outside government, which are usually part of ongoing advisory committee or councils.
- Contributory partnerships: Government funds or sponsors a group, but has no decision-making power or other involvement.
- Operational partnerships: Government arranges to share work but not decision-making power and usually contributes the bulk of the funding.
- Collaborative partnerships: Each partner exercises power in the decision-making process. Shared arrangements can include pooling of

resources such as labor, money, and information. A substantial amount of coordination is required.

Partnerships can evolve from one category to another.

Because government is engaging more frequently in public consultations, many facilitators now specialize in the field of government consultation processes. Their professional association in the US is the International Association for Public Participation. To ensure ethical behavior within the profession, and to contradict the criticism that they facilitate the kinds of participation found at the lower levels of Arnstein's Ladder of Participation, the IAPP has developed guidelines for public participation (see below). These are sensible guidelines to follow if you are organizing a public consultation process and want to build trust.

International Association for Public Participation's Core Values of Public Participation

- The public should have a say in the decisions about actions which affect their lives.
- Public participation includes the promise that the public's contribution will influence the decision.
- The public participation process communicates the interests and meets the needs of all participants.
- The public participation process seeks out and facilitates the involvement of those potentially affected.
- The public participation process involves participants in defining how they participate.
- The public participation process provides participants with the information they need to participate in a meaningful way.
- The public participation process communicates to participants how their input affected the decision.

International Association for Public Participation
http://www.iap2.org/practitionertools/index.html

Power is central to the motivation and aspirations of all members of a TS. In Chapters 7 and 9 you will find tools and specific processes to deal with power issues.

CHAPTER 5

The Tri-Process Model for TS Organizational Effectiveness

Great things are not done by impulse,
but by a series of small things brought together.

Vincent van Gogh

Once your TS moves into Phase 5, the organization-building phase, you are in the process of creating the architecture of a new system or organization. As you would for any organization, you create a structure by developing processes (how work gets done), including policies (general principles to follow) and procedures (specific actions and guidelines). A sustainable infrastructure for a TS can be as simple or complex as the situation warrants.

When I described this phase in Chapter 3, I talked about the different design principles that could underpin the structure of an organization, rather than going into the specifics of what building blocks are necessary. In this chapter I present those building blocks in the form of a process model that is ultimately designed to create a Design Principle 2 (DP2) organization. I recognize that you may need to create a Design Principle 1 (DP1) organization for some reason, or you may be intervening in a laissez-faire organization, but even a DP1 organization needs effective decision-making processes for its leadership. Feel free to use any part of this model and the toolkit in the next chapters to help you create a more effective and healthier TS based on either design principle.

Many academics and government experts exhort community developers, health promoters, and private sector managers to collaborate with situation-appropriate partners. Although some inter-organizational systems, such as industry councils, have been around for many years, there are few primers that explain how to do what the experts are urging. The few experts who do give some directions often focus on only one part of the process (such as governance) and ignore the other processes components. This stumps people trying to implement these new group processes.

The Tri-Process Model

The model of TS organizational effectiveness I present here consists of three process streams components, like the three legs of a stool (see Figure 6.1): trust-building or people processes, governance or power processes, and coordination or management processes. A group builds a new TS organization through conversation and by making decisions about the various options available to them at choice points along the way. Those choice points need to be articulated in a conceptual model so the decisions that are made build a solid foundation and structure for an effective TS. All three legs — trust-building, governance, and coordination processes — need to be addressed. If a stool is missing a leg, it will fall over when you try to use it. In the same way, a TS will be less effective if it is missing one of these process components.

For example, in my experience in the non-profit sector, the trust-building processes are often postponed as a waste of time and energy while the group moves forward on its task. Things may proceed smoothly until group members meet their first challenge, usually a situation rooted in people issues such as conflict or declining energy and interest. If it has not established an adequate level of trust to be able to move through and resolve conflict, the group often slides into decline and member abandonment.

This three-legged model is a tool to help you build just enough structure for the needs of your TS. Figure 2.1 in Chapter 2 showed the different types of TS

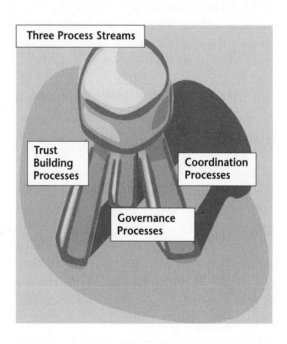

5.1: *Three Process Streams*

along a continuum from the loosest to the tightest structure. If your TS is a coalition or is to be used only for consultation purposes, you may need no more than terms of reference (governance); a few exercises, such as icebreakers, and a value discussion (trust building); and explicit processes for working together and communication (coordination). You do not need an external consultant to facilitate the trust-building exercises (although that is ideal), but the TS leadership and staff do have to set aside the time in meeting agendas for the exercises and provide the leadership to work through them. If your TS is more complex — perhaps it has many members or is addressing a complex problem set, or there is a history of friction amongst TS members — you'll probably need to invest more time and energy in building trust. Some TSs spend the money to hire a neutral facilitator for every meeting, even after the vision phase is completed. Others schedule periodic check-ins or group-building sessions with a neutral consultant to ensure that what was agreed to in the strategic plan is being implemented.

Trust-building process

I call the first leg the trust-building process. It consists of tools and processes to build relationships among the people participating in the TS. It recognizes and encompasses group development theory and also what is known to date on the development of large groups.

Many TS members are reluctant to participate in the processes necessary to build common ground, vision, and trust that will make it easier to work together. They are highly motivated and want to make the change that inspired them to participate in the TS, but they consider process a waste of time. However, it is only through the conversation and discussion that occurs in meetings and in structured group exercises that people can express what their organizations are about and, in the process, build trust that lets them know they will be heard and their needs respected. A getting-to-know-you process and an honest exploration of what we can do with and for each other is the first step to building the desire to work together. All along the TS development journey, trust has to be renegotiated, explored, and reaffirmed in order for the human elements of a TS to work in sync and harmony.

Governance process

The second leg is the governance process. It consists of tools and processes to deal with the power relations of the TS and to answer such questions as: Who in the TS has the power to make decisions? Who are decision makers accountable to? How do the constituencies, stakeholders, and organizations of origin get to provide input and be informed of the activities of the TS?

Many TS participants are not empowered by their organizations of origin to make decisions, and assumptions about power can be lethal to the TS's survival. By addressing power issues explicitly, the TS takes advantage of what is both its strength and its Achilles' heel: the democratic power structure.

Coordination process

The last leg is the coordination process. It consists of tools and processes to coordinate the work of the TS. In the early stages of development, a TS needs an investment of energy to communicate its desire to work in partnership and to secure the buy-in of originating organizations. Once members agree to a common vision and reach agreement on the work of the TS, even more coordination is necessary when resources are shared and intense collaboration begins.

In my community, most funders, while encouraging the development of TS processes, began by denying the need for coordination. Then they progressed to requiring that TS processes be sustained using the existing resources of member organizations. This was unrealistic and discouraged many from participating in the TS process. Funders are now beginning to acknowledge and budget for the coordination necessary for effective TS functioning.

The level of coordination required for a TS is extensive, as are the tools and high-level project-management skills that ensure the participation of many autonomous organizations. Contrary to what some funders have believed, the coordination and collaboration processes are labor-intensive, and the coordination role and functions must be addressed if anything is to be accomplished.

How to Use the Model

This tri-process model provides a developmental framework that coordinators and leaders can use to assess and prioritize their action steps when developing a TS. The three legs of the model can be applied throughout the six phases of the developmental period, but are most necessary in the operational phase (Phase 5). There may be constraints, or development of one process leg may be delayed until another part of the process is complete, but for optimum TS functioning and to create the architecture of a successful TS, it is necessary to integrate all three process legs. My experience with almost 20 TS processes has led me to adopt this three-legged model so that I can quickly assess, wherever I am, what the next step in any leg may be.

I have chosen not to create checklists of necessary steps because all TSs are different, with different needs. However, Figure 5.2 gives an overview of what needs to be done in each leg of the model to ensure all three areas are addressed, no matter what the developmental stage. The tools identified are not necessarily linked or dependent upon each other, but are suggestions for ways you can work on all three organizational legs while building the TS structure. You can pick and choose what is needed for your situation.

5.2: A Descriptive Chart of the Tri-Processes

Developmental Phase	Trust-Building Processes	Coordination Processes	Governance Processes
Phase 4	Getting to know each other	Value proposition: What business are we in?	Where does our power come from?
	Inclusion and exploration of values and individual/ organization goals	What will we produce or what services will we provide? How will we serve the need we have gathered together to address?	What is our mandate and where does it come from? Who do we represent? How can we do that over the life of the process?
Phase 4	Strategic planning Building commitment to goals	Strategic planning What is our work going to be?	Strategic planning What do we want to do with our power?
Phase 5	Organizational structure	Logic model	How are we accountable? Decision-making and authority structure. Terms of reference constitution/bylaws
Phase 5	Boundary setting	Work process design	Roles and responsibilities Decision maker/ staff boundaries
Phase 5	Maintaining focus on goals Mobilizing energy and resources	Marketing plan and systems Financial plan and systems	Policy development ▪ Financial ▪ Human resources ▪ Marketing/communication ▪ Programming
All Phases	Facilitating problem solving and emergent issues	Communication plan and systems	External communications
Phase 5	Conflict management and effective decision making. Building teams and organizational resilience	Ongoing work planning and prioritization	Continuous environmental scanning and adaptation to external trends and events
Phase 6	Evaluation	Evaluation	Evaluation

The three-legged model can be applied to every phase of the development cycle. However, as you can see in the chart, it is most useful in Phases 4 and 5 of the development framework. I also want to show the interdependency of the various steps and emphasize the importance of including trust-building, coordination, and governance processes in the developmental process. Often TS members are so frustrated with previous partnership efforts that went nowhere that they eagerly move ahead on their task, quickly developing an action strategy and postponing until later the activity necessary to create a group strong enough to continue and sustain its work over the long haul. But as I stated before, if trust is not built and there is not yet a genuine interest in one another, at the first sign of conflict or adversity the group will not have the emotional capital to deal with the challenge.

For any group of people, getting to know one another is a step in learning how to trust and work together. It is an indispensable step for a TS. A new culture must evolve out of the interactions of all the members of the group. It is not the same as a new employee joining an established work group with an established culture of unspoken rules and norms, which the employee can, by careful observation ascertain and gradually assimilate. When a TS begins, there are no norms or organizational guideposts. They must be developed, and this can only be done by the members through conversation and trust building, which I discuss in more detail in the next chapter. I will cover governance in Chapter 7 and coordination in Chapter 8.

CHAPTER 6

Trust-Building Processes

The more companies engage in joint ventures, partnerships,
integration — vertically or horizontally — the more culture
and subculture become an issue, and the more
important it is to understand them.

Edgar Schein[1]

Trust-building processes are used to help build relationships among the individuals who come together to form a new group. They create a sense of ownership of the group and ensure that all the participants feel they belong to the group and are included. They include exercises to encourage conversation that may lead to a deeper dialogue between members. These processes are used to build a foundation of trust so that participants willingly share information, make decisions, and accomplish tasks that lead to the completion of goals. Facilitators, organization development consultants, and trainers use them to foster good group process and to encourage people to learn and take the personal risks necessary for change.

Why is Trust Building Important?

Unfortunately, when a group is starting out, trust building is often considered the least valuable process in group development. Group members have sometimes told me, "We are all professionals with good communication skills. We don't need to get to know one another." In these situations, I agree that many of us are professionally trained, but I emphasize that we are still emotional beings who fear, distrust, and need to feel accepted. Without setting aside the time and establishing a safe place to get to know one another, we will not overcome the natural barriers of distrust and anxiety that people feel when engaging with one another outside the comfort zone of their regular daily boundaries. Everyone comes to a new group with preconceived notions, suspicions, and assumptions. Trust-building processes can draw out and deal with these unspoken assumptions and help establish a climate of honesty and openness.

Trust is an essential foundation for all aspects of participation and partnership. Without trust, decisions won't be made, work will not get done, and all the joy and fun of working together will be drained from the group.

The field of organization development is devoted to the study of group process. Academics in organizational sociology and psychology have solid research on how to develop groups more effectively. They have found that people do not have to like each other to work together effectively, but they do have to be able to trust each other. Building trust is not something to skip over.

When we are developing a TS, we are still developing a group, even though it is a group with disparate membership and a diffuse power structure. Trust-building processes are an even more important part of the developmental process for a TS, with its horizontal structure and permeable boundaries between member organizations. It takes a lot of trust to cooperate with former (and current) competitors.

The structure of a TS consists of agreements by participants that are translated into policies and procedures. Without a basis of trust on which to make decisions, there is no impetus to move forward and develop the necessary agreements on how to act as group and an organization. Stalemate is reached quickly. I have found that it is impossible to develop a TS without using trust-building processes. The time devoted to meetings and face-to-face interaction is often too short and infrequent to foster any significant relationship and trust building.

Researchers and practitioners in group processes have developed thousands of tools to facilitate trust-building processes in groups, some of which are presented in the following pages. You should explore others listed in the bibliography or shelved at your local library. Search for books with subjects like organization development, group process, or team building. The important thing is that you know these tools exist and can be incorporated into every stage of TS planning.

Objectives and Tools for Trust-Building Processes

The organizational objectives of trust-building processes include:

+ Building new relationships
+ Building trust
+ Developing a common language
+ Building a common vision and goals
+ Building an effective group that works together on desired outcomes
+ Developing group members in their roles as group members, decision makers, and task workers
+ Valuing and accepting members' emotions and individual perspectives
+ Balancing the natural task focus of the group with attention to group process

Some of the tools you can use to accomplish these objectives are:

- An understanding of group-building process
- Icebreakers, check-ins, and check-outs
- Value discussions
- Visioning and strategic planning processes
- Dialogue
- Adult education principles
- Roles of group members
- Social events
- Storytelling and myth building
- Process consulting

Trust-building processes build a group's culture. Organizational culture is the catchall term for a group's values, beliefs, norms, and assumptions about the world. A new TS must build a new culture that includes aspects of all the cultures it is evolving from. If you incorporate opportunities for reflection and learning, you permit and encourage TS members to examine and explore their originating organization's culture and make conscious decisions about what parts of it are appropriate for them to bring to, or adapt for, the emerging culture of the new TS. Because culture is a group phenomenon embedded in the belief system of its members, the tools to explore it are almost all group discussion-type tools

An understanding of group process is helpful

In 1965, Bruce W. Tuckman developed a model of the four stages of group development (see Figure 6.1). This is the most widely known model of group development and is solidly accepted by organization and community developers around the world. Although the stages are laid out in a linear manner, most group process specialists feel the form of group development is more of a spiral, with the phases repeated over and over during the life of a group. The value of this model is that it shows that group life evolves over time, that conflict is part of process, and that when conflict is worked through, the group learns to work together productively and harmoniously. As well, no

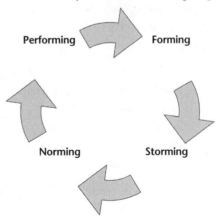

6.1: *Tuckman's stages of group formation graphic*

group goes automatically from birth to high performance without moving through the developmental phases.

Various processes and events take place within each stage. During forming, formalities are preserved and members are treated as strangers. This is a time for:

+ Testing and forming dependence
+ Understanding the environment
+ Learning which behaviors are un/acceptable

During storming, members start to communicate their feelings, but they probably still view themselves as part of their parent department/ organization rather than part of the team. They attack others' insular attitudes while guarding their own. This is a time for:

+ Testing and forming dependence
+ Understanding the environment
+ Learning which behaviors are un/acceptable
+ Intra-group conflict
+ Individuals jostling for position
+ Developing roles

During norming, people feel part of the team and realize that they can achieve work if they accept other viewpoints. This is a time for:

+ Development of group cohesion
+ Acceptance of fellow members
+ Developing unity of purpose

When the group is performing, it works in an open and trusting atmosphere. Flexibility is the key and hierarchy is of little importance. This is when:

+ A vision with clear goals and objectives is complete and is guiding day-to-day work.
+ Group members are clear about their roles and how they are related to the group's objectives.
+ Group members are willing to challenge the nature of relationships within the group and adopt changes as needed.
+ Group members allocate specialized functions to those with appropriate skill sets.

For more information on the stages of group development, check out <http://www.mapnp.org/library/grp_skll/theory/theory.htm> and <http://www.gmu.edu/student/csl/5stages.html>.

Icebreakers, check-ins, and check-outs

This tool, which might be called an icebreaker, a warm-up, or an introductory exercise, is important to help create a safe, welcoming climate for learning and group work. It allows you to build authentic relationships and welcome emotions into group life.

Icebreakers are used at the beginning of a meeting or a workshop to introduce participants to one another and to help people get to know one another. On a more psychological level, they are used to reduce the fear and anxiety prevalent amongst members of a new group. For an established group, they are used as a check-in so people can see how everyone is feeling and to help them transition into the group from whatever they were doing before they arrived. The group leader poses an icebreaker question to the group. Usually the group leader shares his or her answer first and then either proceeds around the circle or asks people to volunteer their answers.

If your group is ongoing, it is good to get into the habit of beginning every meeting with an icebreaker. Use a different question each time. Once a group is established and members know each other well, feel free to adopt a check-in that asks people how they are or what's been going on in their lives. If it turns out that someone needs support or has something stressful going on, other members can make allowances for that person and can pick up the slack. Sometimes that 20-minute check-in prevents members' emotional baggage from contaminating the group process.

The same holds true for check-outs. If the meeting has been stressful, a check-out can let you leave the emotions in the room.

Create icebreaker questions based on the following examples:

- What phrase, motto, or nickname best describes you?
- Where were you brought up?
- Where are your ancestors from?
- Describe the three jobs in your whole life that you've enjoyed the most (paid, full time, part time, or volunteer). What do you see as the common thread that connects all three?
- When did you first realize you were different in some way that was difficult for you?

Create check-in questions based on the following examples:

- Name something that has turned you on recently.
- Tell us something that we wouldn't know or even guess about you.
- What issue or concern is on your mind at this time?

You can also check in using an appreciative inquiry approach, which focuses on strengths instead of weaknesses. Example questions are:

+ What's going right? (Instead of asking what's going wrong.)
+ What's exciting in your life?

Create check-out questions based on the following examples:

+ When I leave here I am feeling _____
+ Tomorrow I hope to feel _____
+ And I hope to get there by _____
+ And I need _____
+ And I wish _____

Value discussions

Values are statements of what we consider important in the way we live our life. We often base decisions on our values. Since they may be emotive, political, and difficult to express, they are frequently hidden. Hidden values create a barrier to group decision making because they make it hard for us to agree, but we are not upfront about why.

TS participants, because of their diversity and lack of shared history, are more at risk of value disagreements than members of a homogeneous group, who are more like than unlike.

Value differences can arise from different lived experiences of gender, sexual orientation, able-bodiedness, class, race, or ethnocultural background. Geerte Hofstede, a Dutch management theorist, identified the "Dimensions of Value Differences" arising from living in different countries. Hofstede recognized that people develop different values based on their different national cultures. Some cultures place a greater emphasis on individualism, while others view collectivism as most important. Members of some cultures prefer having a good distance between themselves and those with political authority. Hofstede also identified a value difference associated with the need to avoid uncertainty. Gender plays a part, with certain cultures traditionally associating particular attributes with masculinity or femininity.[2]

The cultural value differences Hofstede identified can affect the expectations TS members bring with them and the way a group operates. For instance, a group composed mainly of women will develop a different value system and culture than a group composed mainly of men. In our multicultural societies, we will often have members who are living in, or have emigrated from, other cultures, and this can mean that we hold different values.

Cultural differences can also lead to disagreement over the value orientation of a TS. You can use these constructs to frame a question that might reveal whether some members' resistance is due to any of these value differences.

My primary assumption while writing this book is that power sharing and collaboration are desirable ends in themselves. Many would say this is an assumption based on my Western cultural values. I agree with this. There are many people from other cultures who are uncomfortable with power sharing — they may have little experience with it or may come from a country with a repressive regime. One of my colleagues intervened in a TS composed of newcomers from a Middle Eastern country. Their purpose in forming a TS was to advocate for and develop an infrastructure for receiving and settling immigrants in their community. My colleague tried to help them build a collective vision, but it was impossible as they all acknowledged one participant as the de facto leader and expected him to make decisions since he was the most educated and had the most status. They were all from the same country, had experienced extreme repression, and therefore expected a large power distance from their leaders. In this case they put an egalitarian power-sharing structure on hold until they could develop more comfort with different values around power.

At the same time, some places are far ahead of North America in terms of opening up government decision-making systems to the citizenry. In Port Alegre, Brazil, a participatory budgeting process that involves thousands of citizens is a perfect example.[3]

I believe that all humans have the capacity to participate in decisions affecting their lives. However, it is absolutely rational for people not to express their opinions until it is perfectly safe to do so. The primary responsibility of facilitators and leaders creating that safe space is to ensure that people are not asked to reveal themselves if what they say will be used against them. If you are working with immigrant or refugee groups, ask participants up front if it is safe to talk openly. If it is unsafe, take other means to mobilize and involve people (for example, you could use anonymous research processes).

If members of your TS come from a variety of cultures, process tools can help overcome the dominant culture's value set by opening up discussion and raising awareness of the minority cultures. Process tools create the safe place where group members can share their emotions, beliefs, and assumptions. They can also lead to better understanding amongst participants. You can encourage acceptance of diversity by:

+ Affirming the ability of those members who may be at risk of marginalization
+ Providing those members with opportunities to participate in the work and assume a challenge

+ Emphasizing that learning comes from on-the-job education and that competence increases by doing and trying
+ Affirming a sense of belonging
+ Valuing multiple perspectives
+ Evoking diverse role models for the entire group
+ Providing constructive feedback through questions rather than judgments

All groups are diverse in one way or another. The chart in Figure 6.2, adapted from Jane Jacob's *Systems of Survival*, identifies the difference between the values of people involved in the for-profit sector and those involved in the government or non-profit sectors. In conversation or, more often, argument, these values underlie expressed statements but are left unarticulated. People engaged in the discussion who hold other values find it almost impossible to comprehend the expressed statements, as the issue being discussed is often not articulated as one rooted in an underlying value.

6.2: *Values of For-profit Systems and Non-profit Systems/Government*

The Commercial Moral Syndrome (For Profit System)	The Guardian Moral Syndrome (Non-profit System/Government)
Shun force	Shun trading
Come to voluntary agreements	Exert prowess
Be honest	Be obedient and disciplined
Collaborate easily with strangers and aliens	Adhere to tradition
Respect contracts	Respect hierarchy
Use initiative and enterprise	Be loyal
Be open to inventiveness and novelty	Take vengeance
Be efficient	Deceive for the sake of the task
Promote comfort and convenience	Make rich use of leisure
Dissent for the sake of the task	Be ostentatious
Invest for productive purposes	Dispense largess
Be industrious	Be exclusive
Be thrifty	Show fortitude
Be optimistic	Be fatalistic
	Treasure honour

(Jacobs,1994)

When I have been at the table with business representatives and public servants, I have observed representatives of both sectors working hard to find common ground. Yet they fail because both sides are unaware that their whole approach to the work they do is supported by different value systems. Public servants are aware that they are there to protect the public interest. When the rules are bent, they know they are opening themselves and the government that employs them to public criticism if something goes awry. Entrepreneurs, on the other hand, consider that those same rules are made to be broken, for it is their ability to push the envelope, connect the dots differently, and innovate that creates new products or services. Failure is not acceptable in the public servant's work life, whereas the entrepreneur accepts it as life's teacher. Jane Jacobs identifies and explore these differences as no one else has.

In groups where there are underlying value differences, it may be more productive to concentrate first on what members have in common by discussing anticipated outcomes — what they would like to see happen at the end of the day — and how they can get there. You may need to use one of the large system intervention tools for vision setting and strategic planning (see Chapter 3).

Visioning and strategic planning processes

Trust can be built during the visioning and strategic planning processes. If your TS uses a netural facilitator who manages the conversation traffic effectively, all voices get heard, not just the usual dominant ones. By hearing diverse, sometimes contentious, opinions and perspectives, participants are engaged in a major learning process in which they can examine many long-held assumptions and beliefs. The chance to engage in this kind of learning without fear of criticism or failure is a rare experience for many in our culture. Trust is what you get when people are allowed to be who they are, express their feelings, and share their experience.

Also, by bringing together the people who will be responsible for implementation, the planning process builds relationships that will form the social capital to move the plan forward.

Ongoing Trust-Building Process Tools

Once the strategic plan has been developed and the implementation has begun, there usually is great momentum and energy applied to the task. This focus is correct, but at the same time, if you can stay aware of the need to look after the emotional needs of the group and its members, the work will sustain itself longer and will be more satisfying, with productive member engagement. Conflicts can be addressed as they arise and will not simmer underneath the day-to-day activity.

Dialogue

My colleague Catherine Bradshaw developed "Guidelines for Dialogue" (see sidebar) for a workshop we presented together. They are appropriate to use as guidelines for ongoing meetings.

Guidelines for Dialogue
- Think of each other as partners and colleagues and treat each other accordingly.
- Suspend assumptions and certainties — hang them out in front of you so that they can be observed and questioned.
- Observe how other comments stir your thinking.
- Don't say what you already know — discover your response as you speak it.
- Observe your thinking.
- Respond to the question, not to the comments of others.
- Stay in inquiry (focus on learning) and out of advocacy (focus on convincing).

(Adapted from the work of David Bohm by Catherine Bradshaw for the "Ideas that Matter" Workshop, November 2001.)

Adult education principles

Although you may say that you are a community developer or a manager, not an educator, the following principles, developed by researchers in adult education and training, can easily be used to inspire organizational learning in a TS.

- Participants come to sessions with knowledge and experience
- Adults learn by doing
- Participants know what they want to learn
- People need to be able to connect the learning with what they are currently working on or with what they already know and have experienced
- People learn in different ways
- Feedback is critical to the learning process

Roles of group members

Another ongoing tool that TS members can use is Robert Bales' "Roles of Group Members" (see sidebar). You can use them as a checklist to ensure there are members who look after each of these functions when your group engages in meeting discussions and decision making. The same person does not have to assume the same function at every meeting. In fact, each member should be able to undertake any and all these roles at any particular time. Ultimately, in a highly functional group, if you recorded the conversation of a group meeting you would find different participants performing all the different roles. If you find in your meetings that most group members just provide opinions (which is what they are trained to do by TV news shows), the decision making will be less optimal than it could be.

Bales' Roles of Group Members

Task Functions

1. **Defines problems.** Group problem is defined. Overall purpose of group is outlined.

2. **Seeks information.** Requests factual information about group problem or methods of procedure. Requests clarification of suggestions.

3. **Gives information.** Offers facts or general information about group problem, methods to be used. Clarifies a suggestion.

4. **Seeks opinions.** Asks for the opinions of others relevant to discussion.

5. **Gives opinions.** States beliefs or opinions relevant to discussion.

6. **Tests feasibility.** Questions reality, checks practicality of suggested solutions.

Group-Building and Maintenance Functions

7. **Coordinating.** Clarifies a recent statement and relates it to another statement in such a way as to bring them together. Reviews proposed alternatives for the group.

8. **Mediating-harmonizing.** Intercedes in disputes or disagreements and attempts to reconcile them. Highlights similarities in views.

9. **Orienting-facilitating.** Keeps group on-track and points out deviations from agreed-upon procedures or from direction of group discussion. Helps group process along, perhaps by proposing other structures or procedures to make group more effective.

10. **Supporting-encouraging.** Expresses approval of another's suggestion, praises others' ideas, and is warm and responsive to ideas of others.

11. **Following.** Goes along with the movement of the group, accepts ideas of others, expresses agreement.

Individual Functions

(These can be both negative and positive.)

12. **Blocking.** Interferes with the progress of the group by arguing, resisting, and disagreeing beyond reason or by coming back to the same "dead" issue after it has been dismissed. Takes up airtime.

13. **Out of field.** Withdraws from discussion, daydreams, does something else, whispers to others, leaves room, etc.

14. **Digressing.** Goes off the subject by leading the discussion in some personally oriented direction or by expanding a brief statement into a long, nebulous speech.

For an in-depth application of Robert Bales' "Interaction Process Analysis," visit
<http://www.cultsock.ndirect.co.uk/MUHome/cshtml/index.html>

Social events

The opportunity to attend social events and network can be one of the primary motivators for volunteers to be involved in a TS. Social events can celebrate success and build good relationships. Hold them often.

Check out <http://www.theplunge.com/> for ideas.

Storytelling and myth building

Often a TS is formed to undertake large systemic change at the community or sectoral level. I often describe what I do as "building the collective self-esteem of a community." Community developers can achieve this by changing the stories people tell about themselves, individually and collectively.

Re-creating myths or widely held assumptions is a process that engages TS group members and all the participants in any endeavor at every meeting and activity. Telling the story of a group is also a way to enroll others in the group and its activities to create change. Storytelling is a valuable skill for catalyzing change. As an organizer, I use stories of what other communities have done, or stories about what the community was able to do in the past, as a way to illustrate that others have done what we are about to do.

Sometimes the most important changes we need to make are in the stories we tell. According to Harrison Owen, the inventor of the large system methodology called Open Space, "What the mythology of an organization is about is the odyssey of transformation. It superficially talks about other things, but what it really images is that 'transformational journey of the collective spirit,' from wherever it was, to wherever it is, and what happened along the way."[4]

When I was a city councilor, I learned that a new immigrant community was about to arrive in my city. I asked myself, "What would happen if a new group of arrivals were welcomed and celebrated for what they would bring to the established community instead of being feared and shunned?" My executive assistant (who was from the same ethnic background as the new arrivals) and I started an outreach committee that was, in effect, a TS that included city hall, a school board, local residents, and service providers. The story created by the TS process was that this newcomer community could help solve community problems rather than becoming a new problem. This story of being welcomed to a community catalyzed the newcomers to work on their issues and build on their strengths. The economic spin-offs were amazing. New businesses were attracted to the area to serve the incoming residents. A win-win story evolved as our boarded-up storefronts were occupied by new ethnic restaurants, and the newcomers' energies were harnessed to help the existing community initiate street and community festivals. Other spin-off projects included encouraging newcomers to sit on existing boards of directors of community agencies, to partner with service providers already providing culture-specific services in other parts of town, to create literacy programs, and to establish personal relationships with decision makers that led to the development of local businesses.

In a nutshell, the task of any TS is to tell a different story than what is currently being told. If people believe they are powerless and living in a down-and-out community, TS members first, and then the community, must begin to believe a different story about themselves. The story has to change to "We are strong and we have the power to change the course of events in our community." The story of how and why the TS came together forms the first pages. The vision and goals are next. The strategic plans, activities, and accomplishments are the body of the story. The moral of the story is always "We can and we will."

Download the storytellers FAQ from <http://www.timsheppard.co.uk/story/>

A storyboard or scrapbook is a tool you can use to orient new members quickly. It can also be used as a brag book for public relations and as a tool to build and foster an organizational culture. To create a storyboard, use a regular scrapbook, insert photo sheets, and include such things as:

* Pictures of all past and present members of the TS
* Documentation on the problem set
* Explanation of why TS members decided to come together
* Mission statement
* Copies of meeting agendas
* Vision and goal statements
* Event programs
* Media articles
* Governance documents like terms of reference and policies

I have seen the same effect achieved by pasting materials on large boards that can be used as a table or wall display.

A newcomer who spends 15 minutes reading this material will have a good idea of the story of your organization.

Process consulting

Process consulting is a powerful tool used by organization development consultants to enhance group effectiveness and address conflict. It helps a group work together more effectively, and its effects can last long after the consultant has departed.

The skills used in process work are quite different from those used in "expertise-based" consulting because the consultant does not intervene in the content of the TS (i.e., discussions of the problem set or strategies to address it), but concentrates on how the TS works. The consultant is not an expert providing recommendations, but rather someone who asks questions, gathers data, and skillfully provides the safe space in which the group can confront the issues that are blocking it from accomplishing its goals. The consultant helps the group to help itself, working with group members to diagnose problems and design remedies. Process consulting in TSs requires an experienced and skilful human system intervener with a knowledge of TS development.

The benefits of using a neutral facilitator and the tool of process consulting are that someone outside the group, trained in group dynamics, can observe and diagnose problems in group functioning that group members may not be aware of. Process consultation can focus on any of the issues arising from, and related to, the developmental process of TS. This includes everything from the composition of membership to the vision setting, ongoing effectiveness of the organization, or the leadership styles of group members.

There are many more tools and much information available to help a TS build trust and healthy group relationships. Much scholarship in the academic fields of organization development, sociology, and social psychology is devoted to the area of healthy group development. Check out the bibliography for additional resources.

CHAPTER 7

Governance Processes

In dwelling, live close to the ground.
In thinking, keep to the simple.
In conflict, be fair and generous.
In governing, don't try to control.
In work, do what you enjoy.
In family life, be completely present.

Tao Te Ching

For the purpose of creating an effective TS, I consider governance processes to be the processes that are focused on using the power mandated to or assumed by the TS. Governance processes are organizational structures, decision-making processes, and communication strategies.[1]

When I discussed Phase 5 of the development framework introduced in Chapter 3, I elaborated on organizational design principles and choices. In this chapter, I will provide more detail on these choices and describe explicit tools for creating a high-functioning and democratic governance framework for a TS.

Because a TS is made up of many members from diverse organizations, it is vital to develop processes that ensure inclusive and effective decision making. People sign on to a vision, and work to develop and implement solutions to a problem, when they are involved in making decisions about the vision and strategic plan. If they are not involved in decision making, they are less likely to commit, personally, to implementing the decisions. As a TS is not usually a hierarchical organization with coercive power to motivate its members to implement an agreed-to course of action, securing their commitment is the only way to motivate a diverse membership to act in concert.

Objectives and Tools for Governance Processes

Organizational objectives may include:

+ Protection of the public interest

+ Conducting regular meetings to facilitate information sharing, decision making, and strategic planning
+ Acquiring data about the problem set, the external environment, and the group's activity to enter into decision making
+ Creating mechanisms for effective decision making and priority setting
+ Creating a structure for organizational policy making
+ Establishing accountability

Some of the tools you may use to accomplish these objectives include:

+ Discussions about power
+ Contracting
+ Terms of reference
+ Establishing roles (for the chair and for members)
+ Policy making
+ Decision making
+ Regular meeting management
+ Conflict mediation
+ Partnership agreements
+ Basic problem solving
+ Accountability

Discussions about power

As I said in Chapter 4, when you start discussions about how to put the vision and strategic plan into operation, you should also discuss how you will deal with power in the TS. If you don't make an explicit decision about power, members will be relying on their differing assumptions, and the result could be distrust and stalemate. To help build a safe space for the discussion, you will need to develop or reconfirm the group's ground rules. (You may want to reread Chapter 4 for a reminder about the mechanisms of power).

You could ask members the following questions to facilitate a group discussion about how you will handle power. Some of the questions will be raised at the beginning of the process, when prospective members are being asked to attend initial organizing meetings. They may also emerge during Phase 4, the collaborative planning stage, when you decide to form a TS and establish its vision and action strategies.

+ What level of involvement should each stakeholder have?
+ What are the influences on the system?
+ Who has the power?
+ Who/What are the drivers in the system?

+ What do I know that gives me power?
+ What do I know that no one else knows?
+ What would I share and what wouldn't I share?
+ What are the supports for sharing knowledge, skills, processes, our motivation/attitudes, knowledge of the environment and its opportunities, organizational cultures, and power?
+ What would make me eager to share my knowledge?
+ Do I risk anything when I share knowledge?
+ How will something emerge as an issue?

When you get deeper into the discussion, some of the following, more focused, governance questions might come up:

+ What is our mandate? Where does our authority come from?
+ What is our purpose? What kind of business are we in?
+ When we make decisions, who needs to participate in decision making? What kind of decisions will we be making?
+ How can we have effective meetings?
+ How do we make decisions? Consensus or majority rule?
+ What is a policy? What do we need them for? When do we make them?
+ Who says we need a policy? Who takes the leadership to develop a policy? How do we make policy?

Contracting

I use the term contracting, not in the sense of a formal written contract, but to describe how people enter into a commitment to participate when you ask them to join you in the TS to deal with the problem or problem set.

Everyone who joins the process must contract to participate and work on the task. Potential members need to know the following details so they can make an informed decision to join or not:

+ The problem or problem set and its boundary/ies
+ The general objectives of the process
+ How they can help
+ Where you are in the process
+ Who the other partners are and whether they have committed
+ Your approach to power and decision making — for example, will there be an equal partnership in decision making or will they have a time-limited advisory role? Is there a governance framework established?
+ Any ideas you have on anticipated outcomes or final product
+ What kind of resources they might be expected to contribute

Contracting begins again whenever one of the major components of the contract shifts or changes. TS coordinators are aware that this can be as frequent as every meeting. Because TS members participate voluntarily, when circumstances change in their lives or their organization's focus, their commitment to the TS may change. As well, new members entering the process need to be informed of where you are in the process and have your expectations of them made as explicit as possible to ensure their ongoing participation and sustainability.

Formal contracts are an option to record members' commitment to the TS process, but they are usually entered into only when funding and resources are on the table. Keep in mind that formal contracts are not a guarantee that the terms will be honored. Everything, always, can be renegotiated. It is good practice to revisit occasionally the assumptions contained in the contract to see if they still hold value for the participants.

Putting the elements of the contract into story form can help the selling process as well as act as a memory device (see the section on storytelling in Chapter 6). For instance, the story of CEDAC in Chapter 10 could be told as "A group of community activists, local politicians, and business leaders came together to revitalize our local economy. Through a series of meetings and broader sectoral consultations, we developed a plan that focused on four areas: developing a unique marketing niche for our city, constructing a new city centre, creating economic support services for small business, and revitalizing our commercial streets by lobbying for a new subway line." The story could go on to report the struggles (for instance, the many lobbying meetings needed to get the subway line) and accomplishments. If I was telling the story to recruit someone to the process, I would finish it with a request: "We need people like you to help bring this vision to fruition. Will you come to our next meeting and explore what you can contribute?" It is a sales maxim that you should always close your pitch or story with a request for action!

Terms of reference

A written terms of reference is a tool that can provide a minimalist operating structure for a developing group. It acts as a constitution and bylaws for an unincorporated body, usually discussing the purpose for which the group was formed, naming who is responsible for coordination and funding, and describing any structure, such as committees and task groups.

The following elements can be incorporated into the terms of reference document:

- Background
- General mandate/purpose of the group
- Specific responsibilities
- Membership

+ Reporting relationship
+ Staffing and resources
+ Meetings (frequency, structure, etc.)
+ Quorum and decision-making process
+ Time frames

A terms of reference document can take a TS into the operational phase. If the TS is incorporated, a constitution and bylaws would be required and would replace a terms of reference. Once funding is received, staff hired, and projects and programming developed, a policy-making structure is usually necessary (in addition to a terms of reference or constitution and bylaws) to provide day-to-day guidance for staff and volunteers. Good policy can replace the need to give supervisors control over line staff and volunteers.

If one of the TS partners is the lead agency and handles all the funding, the TS may choose to adopt the policy framework of that agency and delegate much of its governance role to this organization and its board of directors. It may be necessary to differentiate some of the governance roles. For example, staff might be covered by the lead agency's HR and financial policies, but the TS would require regular financial and staffing reports.

Establishing roles

It is helpful to have written descriptions of members' roles. This gives you a training and socialization tool that empowers all members by letting them know what their responsibilities are in the TS. Written role descriptions are useful when new members join. It is also relatively easy for members to refer to them when there is conflict or when you are discussing a course of action that will bring new responsibilities to the group. If an executive committee is formed and given some decision-making authority, draft role descriptions for each executive position.

These descriptions will change over time depending on the complexity of the TS. As more money comes in and new projects are developed, the roles and responsibilities will become more sophisticated. All policy and governance documents are living documents, and you should incorporate regular review of them as a matter of course.

The following are suggestions for TS role description that you could include in your TS's terms of reference and in any orientation manual or process. You should draft your own role descriptions, based on the reality of your TS, and include them in your ongoing documentation.

The chair:

+ Manages agreements between organizations
+ Has some formal authority to make decisions between meetings (spell

out what it is)

* Ensures records of agreements, decisions, finances, and transactions are kept
* Understands the value of facilitation at critical choice points
* Mediates the needs of members and their organizations of origin and broader TS goals
* In the absence of support staff, may need to coordinate the work of the group between meetings

The member:

* Supports the chair by asking clarifying questions
* Reads minutes and agendas
* Volunteers for follow-up activity including ongoing task groups
* Participates in visioning or strategic planning
* Participates in decision making and understands decision-making parameters imposed by his or her organization of origin
* States boundaries and asks for what the member and his or her organization need from the process

Questions and answers on policy making

What is a policy?

A policy articulates the principles (values), approach, protocols, and procedures to address a particular issue. To intervene on a policy level means that you are attempting to influence the behavior of a system to achieve desired objectives. Policies are also a means to regulate the use of authority in the absence of the ultimate decision maker. That decision maker may be one person or a senior management team in the example of a hierarchy DP1 organization, or the collective membership that shares power in a DP2 organization. Policies are used to guide future decision making by individuals or sections of an organization.

What do we need them for?

Policies tell the group how members (past and present) have agreed to achieve objectives using the resources available.

When do we make them?

You should consider drafting a policy when an event occurs, or a question arises, that is likely to happen again and either staff or TS members need to systemize or standardize how to deal with it. Policies address things like who can be a member or who you will accept funding from. As soon as the TS hires staff, it is wise to have human resource policies.

Who says we need a policy?

Anyone can raise the need for a policy at a decision-making meeting, but the group must approve the need.

How do we make policy?

The group decides (using either consensus or majority rules) at a regular meeting to adopt a policy. Usually staff or a subcommittee prepares a draft policy that can be discussed at a regular meeting.

What is in a policy?

+ *Purpose.* Why do you need a policy? (This may refer to broad principles or the legislative authority that requires such a policy.)
+ *Goals and objectives.* What do you want the policy to accomplish?
+ *Principles and values.* What principles and values are guiding the design and application of the policy?
+ *Define the problem.* Is there a specific problem that is happening or is anticipated? If so, make it explicit (e.g., "In order to have checks and balances over the spending of money in this organization, we will require two signatures on every check.")
+ *Definition.* Define any technical terms and how the policy is to be carried out.
+ *Procedures.* Include detailed expectations and commitments for each objective.
+ *Accountability.* Spell out who has the role of enforcing the policy. What consequences will there be if someone does not comply with the policy? Identify an appeal mechanism if possible.

See the sample conflict-of-interest policy in the sidebar.

Decision-making tools

Before you make a decision, you need to assemble information about the topic or problem. This can be done by brainstorming, group discussion, working through a formal problem-solving process, or taking a go-around-the-circle approach in which all members take their turn building the collective knowledge of the issue. The group can keep going around the circle, raising questions and issues and taking positions, until the topic is exhausted or there is agreement that more information is needed before a decision can be made.

You can make decisions by consensus (see the sidebar "Consensus Decision-making Process") or by majority rule (see the sidebar "Majority Rules Decision-making Process"). Whichever approach you decide to use, it is important that you record the choice in the TS's terms of reference or bylaws (bylaws are used with incorporated groups) and then stick with that decision.

Sample Conflict-of-Interest Policy for XYZ TS

Purpose: The XYZ TS must strive to be above suspicion. So far as possible, members must avoid the appearance of impropriety in any actions and relationships. Members of the board, volunteers, or staff members of the XYZ TS should disclose any possible conflict of interest they are aware of.

Goal and objectives: The goal of this policy is to clarify the situations when conflict-of-interest rules and procedures apply. In those situations when a conflict of interest may exist, the policy spells out the course of action a XYZ TS member should take to manage the situation in a manner that is fair to all parties.

- The first objective is to prevent the actual occurrence, or perception, of wrongdoing on the part of the organization or any of its members.
- The second objective is to ensure that no member of the XYZ TS shall derive any personal profit or gain, directly or indirectly, by reason of his or her participation with the XYZ TS.
- The third objective is provide a mechanism and guidelines in the event that a member or staff person presents a potential conflict of interest

Principles and values: Serving on the XYZ TS and in the non-profit sector carries with it important ethical obligations. Non-profits and XYZ TS serve the broad public good, and when board members fail to exercise reasonable care in their oversight of the organization, they are not living up to their public trust. In addition, board members have a legal responsibility to assure the prudent management of an organization's resources.

The Problem: This policy is meant to address the sources of most potential conflicts for TS members and staff, arising as a result of affiliation with:

- An organization that has, or is negotiating, a business relationship with the XYZ TS
- An organization seeking funding or other support from XYZ TS

Procedures:

- Full disclosure: Members and staff members in decision-making roles should reveal their connections with groups doing business with the organization. This information should be provided annually.
- Member abstention from discussion and voting: TS and staff members who have an actual or potential conflict of interest should not participate in discussions or vote on matters affecting transactions between XYZ TS and the other group.
- Member abstention from decision making: TS members and staff members ☞

who have an actual or potential conflict should not be substantively involved in decision making affecting such transactions.

Accountability: When any such interest becomes a matter of XYZ TS action, such individuals shall remove themselves from the discussion and abstain from voting. The minutes of all actions taken related to the matter will clearly reflect that these requirements have been met. Failure to make member interests known in items for decision before the TS may result in expulsion from the organization and a motion of censure. ∎

The following are some sample criteria for a member selection policy. As an exercise, use them and other material in this book to draft your own member selection policy.

Prospective members should:

- Have an organizational interest or mandate in the focus of the TS
- Represent a constituency that has a stake in the issue
- Have group process skills
- Have resources to contribute
- Allow the TS to achieve balance between major sectors

Regular meeting management

Meetings are expensive activities. Consider how much it costs to organize meetings (i.e., labor costs, rental costs, paper costs, lost-work costs) and how much you can or cannot get done in them. This is why you should take meeting management seriously.

- **Develop an agenda.** If themes or areas of interest emerge, use them to create a regular agenda format. Always include a section for introductions at the beginning of the meeting, because TSs often have new people representing member organizations. Remember to provide an overview of the group, its work, and its history for these new members. Developing the agenda at the meeting may facilitate more ownership by the group, but it also takes up time. Whether you do this or not depends on the level of trust in the group. If the TS has an extensive decision-making agenda, you can identify items by their importance or by the fact that a decision is required. Often non-profit groups fail to prioritize decisions, and the result is that much of the meeting time can be spent on trivial items. If agenda items don't require a decision, label them "For Information Only" and just ask the group if there are questions or concerns about them.

Consensus Decision-making Process

You would use a consensual decision-making model to ensure that all perspectives around the table are expressed, heard, and integrated into decision making.

In this process, a motion or a specific course of action is framed and placed before the group. The chairperson can test to see if agreement has been reached by posing the question "Do I have agreement?" Members express their support of, or concerns with, the proposed course of action. Members are also empowered to block the proposed course of action by stating they cannot allow the group to proceed because of their concerns. If members have expressed concerns but choose not to prevent the group from moving forward with the action, they can state that their concerns have been heard and that they will allow the group's decision to move forward.

The chair can test for consensus by asking group members to raise their hands to signify agreement. You can also raise hands halfway up or down. Halfway indicates "maybe," weak compliance, some reservations, or not quite sure. This process is empowering for the group because it doesn't ask for yes or no commitments, but allows for maybes and ifs, and signals more information, more ideas, and more discussion are necessary before the group can reach a decision.

Variations on the Theme

Ask for alignment rather than agreement. This allows those not in agreement to give it a try, but allows the group to revisit the issue if it does not work out.

If the consensus decision-making process becomes stalemated, you can attempt to release the stuck energy by cycling back to the central intention of the TS. By going back to first principles — your vision or your purpose in coming together — you get people to raise their sights out of the present to an ideal.

Another way to move forward is to get the group to agree, as part of its decision-making process, to allow the chairperson to make the decision and move the group forward. The chair must use good judgment to discern whether the group needs more time to explore options or to access more information.

Another way to place a boundary around the time allowed for consensus discussion and decision making is to obtain agreement at the onset of discussion that the decision must be reached by a certain time and that the chair has a veto that carries the responsibility to move the group forward if necessary. Many groups proceed on a consensus model, but if there is a conflict they revert to the majority rules decision-making process. If this is what your group decides to do, it should be formalized in the terms of reference or bylaws so that everyone is clear about the process.

Majority Rules Decision-Making Process

The majority rules decision-making process is also known as parliamentary procedure. It is the decision-making system in which a vote is taken, and everyone allowed to vote expresses his or her opinion on the motion by voting. The amount of time given for discussion is usually limited at the discretion of the chair. 50 percent of the votes cast plus one results in a decision.

Rules of Order for Formal Meetings

Rules of order are designed to allow group participants to participate in decision making in a formal manner. They have evolved out of the rules that govern parliaments and developed from the British political tradition. Robert's Rules of Order are one version — and they can be disempowering for those not versed in them.

The main steps in the decision-making process under majority rules are:

- A proposal or motion is introduced by its sponsor or mover
- A specific motion is made
- The motion is seconded by another member who supports it
- The motion is discussed, with discussion controlled by the chairperson
- The motion may be amended before a decision is taken on the motion as a whole
- The meeting makes a decision by voting on the motion (as presented or amended)
- If the motion is defeated, a related motion can be considered or the meeting can move on to consider other business

Variations on the Theme

To move closer to the ideal of consensus decision making, a group can require a supermajority of 75 percent for a motion to pass.

Minutes. Designate someone to take minutes. They do not need to be extensive — you don't have to record every word that every person says — but they are needed to keep track of decisions made by the group.

If the meeting is more facilitated than chaired, be sure to type up the data that is entered on flip charts during discussion. A facilitated meeting is led by someone who is neutral. A trained facilitator will use techniques like posing a question to the group and recording the input on a flip chart. (A chairperson is never neutral and, even if she or he does not have a vote, is empowered with some decision-making and representative authority. Often a chairperson will vet the minutes before they are released to a group's members to ensure that his or her interests are protected in the record of the meeting.)

Establish ground rules for meetings. You don't need to develop new ground rules every meeting, but it pays to have a few basic ground rules that can be used for most of your meetings. These rules contain the basic ingredients needed for a successful meeting. The "Guidelines for Dialogue" (included in the "Ongoing trust-building process tools" section of Chapter 6) are great to use as ground rules. Keep them posted at all times.

Strategic planning. Whenever a decision is made, make a habit of discussing resources, time frames, and volunteer/s needed to implement it. Even if your TS has paid staff, they are almost always overworked and there may be someone who is eager to assume a specific task. Ask and you shall be surprised.

Time management. One of the most difficult facilitation tasks is time management — time seems to run out before tasks are completed. Therefore, the biggest challenge to maintaining a TS's momentum is to keep the process moving. The chair might ask attendees to help keep track of the time.

Evaluating the overall meeting. Leave five to ten minutes at the end of the meeting to evaluate the meeting process. Have each member rank the meeting on a scale of one to five, with five indicating the meeting ran smoothly, and have members explain their rankings. Ask the people with the most influence to rank the meeting last. If process issues emerge, put them first on the next meeting's agenda.

Closing meetings. Always end meetings on time, and attempt to end on a positive note. At the end of a meeting, review actions and assignments, set the time for the next meeting, and ask each person if they can make it or not (this will get them to make a commitment).

For more information on meeting management, check out
<http://www.mapnp.org/library/misc/mtgmgmnt.htm>.

Conflict mediation

Conflict is inevitable in a TS. Each member has differing needs and interests as an individual and as part of a member organizations. As well, you have a mix of personalities, and many people have previous history with each other. It is foolhardy to assume that conflict can be avoided. Instead, welcome it by bringing differences to the surface, regarding those differences as natural, and then focusing on finding common ground. The differences need to be clarified and understood by all.

If you can not easily resolve the conflict through a basic problem-solving process (see the section later in this chapter), group members can either agree to disagree or they can agree to develop a sidebar process to further explore the issue. In a sidebar conflict-resolution process (Open Systems theory calls it a "rationalization of conflict") the parties involved in the conflict agree to move it aside so the main work of the meeting can continue. To move a conflict aside, the parties must agree to a time and place to resume their conversation. They can have the facilitator present if they wish, and often they will record the conversation. The recording allows others to review the thinking processes of parties involved in the conflict. If the people in conflict can agree to a course of action, they are invited to bring the resolution back to the main meeting.

Once the conflict is accepted and explored, the TS can move forward with its agenda rather than getting mired in trying to pretend there is no conflict. In addition, the conflict itself can raise new ideas and energy for the TS to consider and adopt.

Conflict is normal. It is how we deal with conflict that makes it a problem. By setting up ground rules for conflict before it emerges, you help normalize it when it does inevitably appear. Additional ground rules might include respecting all parties' opinions; keeping the focus on the ideas or the behavior, not the personalities; letting people finish speaking before interrupting; and/or setting aside time and space to explore the conflict without derailing the meeting agenda.

Partnership agreements between TS members

You will need to decide whether formal partnership agreements are necessary for your TS. The need for an agreement is usually determined by the amount of resources a partner contributes and by the partners' requirements for formal documentation. If an agreement is necessary for one partner, all TS member organizations must be a party to it and sign the agreement. As a general rule, the larger the partner organization is, the more likely it will require a formal agreement before it makes a financial commitment. You may need legal advice to ensure that the agreement would stand up in court.

If you don't need a legal document, you can draft an informal partnership agreement that could include the following details about the TS:

- Principles, beliefs, and values
- Objectives and expected outcomes
- Roles
- Responsibilities
- Benefits and acknowledgments
- Process objectives/Values
- Mechanisms for conflict resolution and evaluation
- Resource contributions

Basic problem solving

Once a TS is operational, it will likely have regular meetings and will deal with problems in a specified manner. The governance tools to deal with problems include policy making and strategic planning, but first you need to explore the problem with a problem-solving process. Basic problem solving involves:

- Gathering the facts
- Defining the problem (90 percent of the solution of any problem lies in its proper definition)
- Identifying the options
- Recognizing the preferred alternative
- Getting community input if needed
- Doing you own thinking
- Weighing each other's viewpoints
- Keeping your focus on the benefits of solving the problem
- Retaining your sense of humor

7.1: *Accountability*

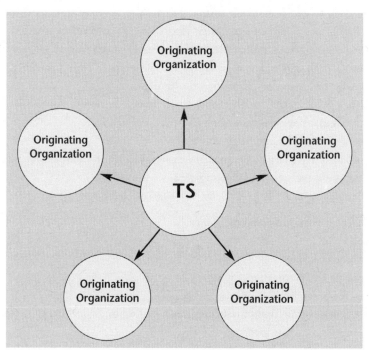

Accountability

Because its power structure is shared between its members as individuals and its members as organizations, a TS has a complex accountability structure. It is obliged to account for its activities to members and organizations of origin (see Figure 7.1). Usually the manner in which it has agreed to report to members is spelled out in a policy.

A policy can require that the TS report to its community in a written newsletter, by e-mail, or at an annual general meeting. The accountability mechanism must be designed by the TS participants and be acceptable to them in order to build the trust that is necessary to become sustainable.

Governance processes provide the structure to undertake the work of a TS, which is information sharing and decision making.

> Accountability is the obligation to answer for the results of authorized actions and for the manner in which responsibilities are discharged.

CHAPTER 8

Coordination Processes

*Opportunity is missed by most because it is dressed in overalls
and looks like work.*

Thomas Alva Edison

The last leg of my organizational effectiveness model for TSs is coordination processes. This set of processes and tools is essential for the work that must occur to form a TS and keep it operating and implementing its vision and strategic plan.

When I was first involved in TS formation in the early 1990s, funders and others in decision-making roles wanted to break down the silos of individual organizations primarily to see if their money could go further and meet more needs, yet they were not willing to give organizations the time and resources they needed to do the work that would ensure inter-agency collaboration. They also refused to acknowledge the massive amount of activity involved in bringing diverse organizations together and developing a plan to work together. This attitude is still pervasive, as program funding guidelines continue to require that non-profits develop a TS before submitting a proposal. As I indicated in Chapter 3, the developmental phase (Phases 1 to 4) can take up two years and requires a lot of up-front energy and resources.

The coordination functions take the form of what is often considered "women's work": helping people feel included, making sure they know about meetings, ensuring they have the information needed to make decisions. And like women's work, these jobs are often unseen and unvalued by society. There is still a strong cultural tendency to pretend this is not high-level work and, therefore, that it does not deserve compensation. My response: If you ignore these jobs, nothing will happen. It *is* work and it is a vitally necessary activity that underpins the success and sustainability of a TS.

Some of the jobs required to coordinate the work of a TS include:

+ Planning
+ Scheduling

+ Allocating
+ Instructing
+ Assembling information for decision making
+ Monitoring actions

Nowadays, much of this work happens online.

Objectives and Tools for Coordination Processes

The organizational objectives of coordination processes include:

+ Program planning
+ Planning and implementing work plans
+ Creating an organizational structure that facilitates working and communicating across organizational boundaries to undertake the task
+ Keeping the group focused and moving forward on its strategic plans
+ Creating and maintaining a communications system
+ Managing the human resources through hiring processes or contracts
+ Financial planning and management
+ Seeking funding through proposal writing

Some of the tools you can use to accomplish these objectives are:

+ Note or minute taking
+ Logic models
+ Work plans
+ Timelines
+ Communications mechanisms (i.e., e-mail, listserv, internal newsletters, meeting agenda packages)
+ Large group meetings
+ Work groups and subcommittees or virtual teams
+ Hiring staff or contracting with a consultant to coordinate the work needed to keep the TS going

Even though these processes are changing because of information technology, they still require intensive time and energy and are critical to the knowledge transformation element of a TS. A TS exists to share knowledge, to give meaning to the information gathered, and to add quality and value to the assembled information, so all this information must be managed and communicated to TS participants. This is done by the written word. It is still the written word whether it travels by e-mail or hard copy, and somebody has to record it and fashion it into an acceptable form for communication and then decision making. This is the work of this leg of the organizational effectiveness model. It begins on Day One and continues past the last day, as someone should keep the records until all the legal requirements for infor-mation storage have passed.

Note or minute taking

Note or minute taking is critical to ensure a memory of what people discussed and agreed upon. Meetings that happen without minutes or notes taken are virtually useless in terms of organization building and moving a process forward. If the des-ignated record keeper or other participants are not skilled at taking notes, consider using a minutes template. Design the template with a space for names of meeting participants and the date at the top of the page, and then number off sections of the template for adoption of the minutes and for each agenda item. Allocate suf-ficient space to each agenda item for the record keeper to note any decisions that are made.

I use the minutes to build understanding and consensus between meetings, and I use recorded discussions as data to insert into planning documents (see the next section).

Logic models

After you've developed a strategic plan, it's good to put together a logic model. This step involves stakeholders in deciding not only program objectives, but also appropriate implementation steps. It allows the group to take the strategic direc-tions and/or goals and develop them into programs and projects with accountabili-ties, indicators, and milestones. Figure 8.1 shows a template for a logic model. At a meeting or brainstorming session, ask members the questions and fill in the boxes with your answers.

Work plans

Most of the large system methodologies described in Chapter 3 focus on getting a group to agree on what it should do, *not* who should do it, how it should be done, and when to do it. All that planning is left for the subsequent detailed work plan, which you should develop as soon as you've decided on your strategic plan.

You will probably want to form subcommittees made up of TS members to develop work plans for the different activities agreed to in the strategic plan. I've listed some examples of the questions such subcommittees should consider, but you should develop your own questions based on your particular situation. For example, if your TS is an advocacy coalition, you might use the questions under "Advocacy Strategy" to guide you through Phase 4 of the TS development framework. Your group's answers, recorded under the questions reworded as headings, will form the group's project, fundraising, or advocacy plan. Once you have developed a work plan, create an implementation plan that sets out who does what.

8.1: *Logic Model*

Logic Model for

Organization (Name) _____

Or Program (Name) _____

Components	Activities	Target Group	Short-term Outcomes	Long-term Outcomes	Indicators
What are the main sets of activities?	What things are done? What services are delivered?	At whom are the activities directed?	Logical, meaningful, measurable benefits to participants/ community	Measurable changes or competencies - changes in behaviour or condition	Measures of success
The number of components depends on the size of your program and how you conceptualize it - it may be just one or many	The things the program staff do, or the services you deliver. The means by which the desired outcome will be achieved.	Individuals, groups. Organizations or communities for whom the programs/ services are designed. May be specified in terms of socio-demographic characteristics	The direct results of the program on its participants. They show why the program will lead to longer term outcomes * to include the direction of change	The consequences of the program in the broader community	Process Evaluation: to improve the operation of the program. Evaluates the components, activities and target groups Outcome evaluation: to assess the impact of the program. Evaluates the short and long-term outcomes

The Centre for Health Promotion, associated with the University of Toronto, offers more information on logic models. Visit its website at <http://www.thcu.ca> to download free resources such as a logic models workbook and slide presentation.

The Urban Institute describes how to create a logic model for use in evaluation at <http://www.bja.evaluationwebsite.org/html/documents/stop1-4.html#chap2>

The W.K. Kellogg Foundation discusses the use of program logic models to measure program impacts at <http://www.wkkf.org/Pubs/Tools/Evaluation/Pub3669.pdf>

A Project Plan

A project plan sets out the activities you must undertake to achieve your program or project goals and objectives. It might include references to fundraising or advocacy plans, which can be developed separately (see below).

Pose these questions to your group in person or via written documents or e-mail and record the answers. When you have a consensus on the answers, you have a project plan.

- What do we want to accomplish?
- What activities or milestones will get us there?
- Who else is doing this work? How will we reduce overlap and duplication?
- How will we promote information sharing and collaboration while maximizing impact?
- What human, financial, and material resources will we need?
- What resources will we be able to get donated or "in kind"?
- What parts of the project may require external support?
- What policies and procedures do we need to review or develop before proceeding?
- How will we ensure the project's integrity is maintained and its outcomes sustained beyond the funding period?
- Who will carry out each part of the project plan?

A Fundraising Strategy

A fundraising strategy sets out the activities you must undertake to raise the funds needed to achieve your program or project goals and objectives. Many of the points addressed in a fundraising strategy should also be considered and agreed to in the project plan. Once all the questions below are addressed to everyone's satisfaction, and the consensus is recorded, you have a fundraising plan.

- Who is the target group for our services or activities?
- What is the catchment area or geographic scope of our program and projects?
- What will be our key activities?
- Who might be interested in funding us?
- Why would our project be attractive to external funders? What are the costs and benefits of funding our initiative?
- How will we make our pitch so as to demonstrate relevance and value to the funders' needs?
- Does our project meet their funding criteria?
- Are we able to comply with the funding process/timetable?

- Who will champion our cause in the initial stages? In the long run?
- Who will actually manage/implement our fundraising strategy?
- What are the keywords that describe our project?
- What human, material, and financial resources do we need?
- What supports are available (i.e., secondments, donated/in-kind goods and services, allocated dollars, etc.)?

Advocacy strategy

An advocacy strategy is used to plan the campaign or lobbying activity needed to achieve your public policy objectives.

- What is the issue we want to address? What are its underlying causes (i.e., if your overall issue is homelessness, you would want to determine why some people do not have homes)?
- What are our goals and objectives?
- Who is our target audience? Who has the power to make the changes we want to see?
- What can we do to draw public attention to this issue?
- Who might be our allies?
- How can we raise money to fund our activity? What groups or individuals might support us?
- Who will implement our advocacy strategy?

You will find that the details of a work plan are always changing in response to events and new information. Although you will discuss and agree on work plans at your meetings, there is often not enough time to plan all the work a TS needs to do, and a new development (for example, a new funding announcement) may require you to devise a new plan or task on the fly.

When I am involved in a TS, I use the time between face-to-face meetings to build documents that change and grow throughout the month. I send out drafts of these documents and invite feedback, then incorporate participants' comments on objectives, options, and decisions taken into the next draft. This gives participants and their organizations time to see in an organized fashion what the group is thinking and where it is at so that they can prepare to react to it or build upon it at the next face-to-face meeting.

Timelines

Everything takes longer than you think — even when you know it does and allow for it! Drawing a timeline is a simple technique to set priorities among activities and events that must be completed to create a partnership or carry out a program.

Follow these steps to create a timeline:

+ Draw a horizontal line on a piece of paper.
+ Graduate it into appropriate blocks of time (days, weeks, months). The first block is the present; the last is the completion date.
+ Think of all the tasks to be completed.
+ Place the tasks on the timeline in the order in which they have to be done. If several tasks must be done at once, place them in order of most importance at that particular time.

Communications mechanisms

As information workers, the material we input into our work process is information. The information comes in via communication channels, and the transformed knowledge goes out via communication channels. In a TS, communication is the main day-to-day work activity for staff and volunteers. You need to determine systematically how the communication work processes are going to be structured. Ask yourselves the following questions and use the answers to guide you in setting up your internal and external communications channels. Some of the external communications issues — such as who will speak on behalf of the TS and who develops the key messages and approves them — should also be addressed in a communication policy.

+ How frequently should we communicate?
+ Who will communicate with whom?
+ What communication channels are most appropriate?
+ What types of information will be shared?
+ What information is proprietary?
+ How will we deal with communication problems?
+ What aspect of our respective corporate cultures might hinder communication?
+ How can we overcome those barriers?[1]

Large group meetings

Organization development consultants often complain that after they have gone in to help a group develop a vision and strategic plan, the plan breaks down in the implementation phase. You can use large group meetings to organize volunteers into smaller groups to develop these plans and assign people to carry out each action. If you don't yet have a broad strategic plan and need to figure out the next steps for your TS, ask the whole group to brainstorm the work needed and organize it into sequential steps, then ask for volunteers for each task or step. Record the steps and tasks on flip charts and list the names of people who have volunteered for each task. This will be your work plan! Be sure to record it in notes or minutes.

Work groups and subcommittees or virtual teams

If the work is extensive and you do not have enough time to tackle the work planning in the large group meeting, consider forming work groups, subcommittees, or virtual teams. If you have decided to delegate planning or the implementation of a task to a subcommittee, make sure that, before they leave the large group meeting, you have a list of volunteers who agreed to participate, the time and place for their meeting, and a decision on how they are going to meet (in person, by teleconference, or via the internet). Be sure to ask one of the subcommittee members to act as liaison with the main group.

The questions in the section on work plans are useful for initiating discussion in this kind of group. They are particularly useful when communicating by e-mail. For e-mail discussions, I assign everyone in the conversation a font color and cut and paste their ideas, comments, and suggestions into the appropriate section of a planning document. All of a sudden themes and agreement start to emerge. I feed back to the group what I see happening to test whether consensus is developing, and if everybody is happy I announce that part of the discussion closed and move on to the next. If you spend a lot of time communicating online, there are virtual team facilitators and sophisticated software you can use to do this kind of work.

Hiring staff or contracting with a consultant

Problems arise when TSs hire staff with specialized knowledge before hiring people with a generalist background. In a TS, the coordination function and skill set are the most important in terms of organizational sustainability and effectiveness. Members of the TS can provide the technical knowledge, but they are usually unwilling or unable to provide the day-to-day support work.

From my many years providing leadership and support to TSs, I have learned that to move a TS forward you need the ability to create and organize a traditional organization, as well as some extra skills. As TSs are a hybrid of existing organizations, the level of complexity exceeds that of a traditional organization, multiplied by the number of partners. When you add to the mix the desire for equal power relations and the task of calming a broad turbulent domain (the task environment outside of a TS), it becomes clear that the person who is the center point of all activity needs a lot more skills than your typical project coordinator.

Generally, the skills and competencies that a TS coordinator needs are similar to the ones possessed by a generalist/manager like a community developer or health promoter in the non-profit sector or a project manager in the private sector. A TS coordinator must possess the following competencies, which are defined as the specific and observable knowledge, skills, attitudes, and behaviors that contribute to doing a job effectively:

+ Analytical thinking
+ Business acumen
+ Ability to lead and manage change
+ Impact and influence
+ Initiative and innovation
+ Results orientation
+ Relationship-building
+ Organizational awareness
+ Financial management
+ Human resources management
+ Issues management
+ Negotiating skills
+ Oral and written communication skills
+ Meeting management
+ Planning and work management
+ Project management
+ Contract management
+ Facilitation abilities
+ Desktop computer literacy
+ Risk-benefit management
+ Coaching skills

If you add content knowledge of the target problem area to the above list, you may be expecting too much. Generally people who are attracted to technical areas are more detail oriented and experience a great deal of frustration when it comes to managing the messy art of relationship building. If you have the luck to find people who can do both, treat them well — they are a rare breed. I have noticed that as funders and senior decision makers support building partnerships with outside organizations, they are expecting their staff with content expertise to take on the job of developing and supporting TSs. This is unrealistic and a critical reason that many TSs are floundering. Instead, to ensure success, look for the competencies listed above when hiring a TC coordinator.

The TS Coordinator

Ensure that a coordinator is assigned to the process by one of the partners or is hired once funding is available.

The work of regular meetings will not happen without someone assuming the coordinator's role. Volunteers rarely fill the role as they do not have the time and ☛

energy to devote themselves to managing a complex process.

During the contracting and design stages, the coordinator's role is a neutral but activist one. In other words, the coordinator must not influence the outcome of vision and strategic plan processes, but must be an activist when it comes to selling the process, recruiting participation, and fostering commitment. Thomas Cummings describes this ability to be a neutral activist as a required skill set when dealing with trans-organizational systems.

Given these role demands, the skills needed to practice TS development include political and networking abilities. Political competence is needed to understand and resolve conflicts of interest and value dilemmas inherent in systems made up of multiple organizations, each seeking to maintain autonomy while interacting jointly. Political savvy can help coordinators manage their own roles and values in respect to those power dynamics. It can help them avoid being co-opted by certain TS members and thus losing their neutrality.

Networking skills are also indispensable to TS coordinators. These include the ability to manage lateral relations among autonomous organizations in the relative absence of hierarchical control. Coordinators must be able to span the boundaries of diverse organizations, link them together, and facilitate exchanges among them. They must be able to form linkages where none existed and to transform networks into operational systems, capable of joint task performance.[2] ■

CHAPTER 9

Lateral Leadership

It is not the critic who counts: not the man who points out how the strong men
stumbled or where the doer of deeds could have done them better.
The credit belongs to the man who is actually in the arena; whose face is marred
by dust and sweat and blood; who strives valiantly; who errs and comes short
again and again; who knows the great enthusiasms, the devotions, and spends
himself in a worthy cause.
Who, at the best, knows the triumph of high achievement; and who,
at the worst, if he fails, at least fails while daring greatly,
so that his place shall never be with those cold and timid
who know neither victory nor defeat.

Theodore Roosevelt

Even if it uses participative tools and structures, a TS requires someone to fulfill leadership functions. However, it is a different kind of leadership than that empowered by title and authority. Most people believe that leadership is exercised when a so-called leader understands a problem, articulates it in plain language, then advocates a plausible solution and is in a position to make a decision or influence the decisions that can be made. When the solution is implemented, the leader directs the activity and resources of group members to carry out the agreed course of action and, if necessary, uses tools based in coercion and control to ensure completion of the task. This is the form of leadership we see in the political arena and, to a greater or lesser extent, displayed by the executives and managers in the governments and organizations where we work.

In a TS, as in a traditional hierarchical organization, there are still problems that need to be identified, visions that must be agreed to, goals to be set, and strategic plans to be implemented. However, in a TS, with its flexible, underorganized system, different people may assume this function at different times. An individual may not necessarily have the title of leader, chairperson, or executive member, but as a member of a TS, he or she is responsible for ensuring that the process moves forward by using the power, resources, and abilities at his or her disposal.

We need to rethink our concept of leadership as something associated only with those people who hold the vision and direct or assign tasks. I consider the primary function of leadership in a TS is to move the process forward. Sometimes that leadership role means making sure the next meeting is held and that members are kept informed. Coordination activity is traditionally considered a support function, but if it does not occur, the TS is as doomed as it would be without a vision or a meeting chairperson. Leaders in a TS are facilitators of horizontal cooperation or, as William Bergquist, Juli Betwee, and David Meuel described it in *Building Strategic Partnerships*, "an integrator of the partnerships function and operations."[1]

Because members of a TS share decision-making power while remaining accountable to the organizations of origin, a TS is not considered autonomous. It has feedback loops to other organizations or a hybrid system of governance. This shared power structure leads to a different form of organizational learning that is, by nature, shared. Shared learning, also called puzzle learning, is based on the premise that no one person holds all the pieces of the puzzle, but by sharing our knowledge we can build a collective picture and solution.[2]

What Kind of Leadership is Required in a TS?

Organizations characterized by power sharing and collective learning require a different kind of leadership. In their book *Getting It Done: How to Lead When You Are Not in Charge*, Roger Fisher and Alan Sharp called it "lateral leadership." Lateral leadership is the opposite of telling others what to do. It involves working with others collaboratively to create a better process for determining solutions. Lateral leadership invites others to participate in identifying and resolving problems. People who practice lateral leadership will pose questions to a group and invite contributions from members in order to put the pieces of the learning puzzle together rather than sharing their perception of the problem and advocating for their preferred solution.

You don't need to have a formal title or leadership position; if you facilitate a discussion and the sharing of learning, and negotiate the manner in which group participants work together, you are providing leadership. These leadership skills may not be recognized as such at the beginning of a TS, especially if members are not used to process-orientated work methods, but it will soon become apparent that they are absolutely necessary to move the group forward.

TSs, with their tendency toward equal power relations and democratic decision making, require this form of shared participative leadership, which integrates rather than separates and controls. Many people would argue that this emerging form of leadership is necessary in just about any modern organization where employees are knowledge workers and know more about their job than their managers do. With their loyalty to professional standards and bodies, each knowledge worker or functional department can be seen to be as much of a silo as an organization is. Such an organization requires a form of leadership that responds to the needs of the situation by managing the available pool of knowledge resources. The pool may be the members of a TS sitting around the table, the human resource pools of all member organizations, or the human resources of a wider constituency or community.

What are the Characteristics of Lateral Leadership?

Lateral leaders can exhibit any of the traditional characteristics we associate with leadership, but in order to foster participation and commitment they will also use facilitative techniques that motivate TS members to reach agreement on strategic plans and undertake tasks. This is in place of the traditional methods of coercion or control, which are used by managers and political leaders to force compliance with a leader's decision.

Some of the specific characteristics of lateral leaders are the following:

- Lateral leaders begin by knowing themselves. They can state what they need out of the process; can share their feelings and represent their organization or constituency; and can understand their own self-interest.
- They are comfortable with human emotions, their own and those of other people. They accept that humans are emotive beings who are motivated, guided, and inspired by their emotions, and they accept self-interest as a principal motivator.
- They empower others by empowering themselves. Lateral leaders can state their own and their organization's needs up front without apology. By stating their boundaries and what they will and won't support, they allow others to emulate their example and help to create an open and honest process.
- They understand that for the task to get done, trust must be built among participants. Trust gets built one day at a time, through honesty, keeping promises, and following through.
- They foster a culture of inclusion and sense of belonging and ownership. Group members must feel at ease and gain a sense of value by belonging to the group. As a result, members don't threaten to leave the group or, worse, actively work to sabotage the process.

- They develop a common language to provide the infrastructure for conversation and dialogue. A lateral leader becomes a bridge across organizational cultures when group members come from different organizational or ethnocultural backgrounds. Since it is not easy to trust someone if you can't understand what they are saying, it is critical to level the playing/learning field by building a common language.
- They can let go of control and process outcomes. A lateral leader trusts that the combined wisdom of a group will imagine a far better solution or plan than one person alone (even the leader) can accomplish.
- They provide structure. This includes structuring meetings by ensuring there is an agenda that focuses on decision-making items and on building the architecture of a new group.
- They understand that structure can be built with tools, such as strategic planning, icebreakers, and participative policy planning. Lateral leaders use effective questioning, instead of advocacy and direction skills, to encourage thinking and learning and to build a broad communication loop.
- They hold the group's vision by building a group myth and culture through storytelling the why, what, when, and how of the group. They foster a learning culture and undertake conflict mediation when necessary.
- They keep the group focused on the goal. Because of the lack of structure and clear power accountabilities in a TS, participants often become anxious. Keeping the group's focus on the goal channels the anxiety into productive work.
- They keep in touch, share information, and resolve problems when they crop up.
- They create opportunities to socialize! Having fun is part of life. Everyone wants to have fun.

You may be saying to yourself, "These characteristics sound good, but what does such a leader look like in real life?" Or perhaps you are wondering how you can become such a leader. Who teaches the process of holding a group vision or letting go of control? What tools or knowledge exist that can help develop lateral leadership skills? What do you have to work with? Well, it's you that is the instrument of change.

In Chapters 3 and 4 I discussed group dynamics — the characteristic of how a group is functioning — and how the dynamic can be improved by a conscious intervention, while in Chapters 6 through 8 I described some of the tools that can be used to change a group dynamic so the group can achieve its task. An intervention can be carried out by one person using a word or even a behavior that results in a change in the group dynamic. When you choose words consciously to change a group dynamic, you are an intervener, yet you are only using the power of your own self to effect this change on the emotional life of a group. To do this you need to know yourself and understand the impact you can have on a group.

The principal tool to help you intervene in a TS is you! In order to practice lateral leadership, you will need to get to know yourself better, make some changes if they seem appropriate, and develop some of the following abilities:

- Identify and share your emotions
- Handle your stress
- Establish boundaries
- Develop negotiation skills
- Develop communication skills
- Become a storyteller
- Accept conflict and learn how to resolve it
- Learn how to influence and persuade
- Use tools

Identify and share your emotions

Emotional awareness is the ability to identify and work with your emotions and feelings. Interventions in which you share your feelings are incredibly powerful. If you model that you have feelings, then others are allowed to have their feelings too. When emotions are freely expressed, they do not sabotage conversation or relationship building. Accepting your feelings as human leads you to accept and honor the emotions of others.

All too often, emotions are not permitted in groups and workplaces because we have a societal norm that states we value rationality above emotionality. As children, we are taught to control our emotions and told that acting or speaking emotionally is manipulative, dishonest, or ignorant.

As a result, people talk around their feelings, project them, use code words, interject red herrings, or say little. You will recognize when this happens during a meeting because you won't have a clue what is being said. However, if group members freely share emotions such as fear, pride, and joy, deeper conversation can emerge and, ironically, more clarity is achieved in decision making.

Many of us did not learn a basic emotional vocabulary. In particular, males generally have been socialized to ignore their feelings and not express them. Men and women who have experienced trauma usually survived it by shutting down their feeling function. The good news is we can reclaim this basic human function through therapy and self-healing. As I went through my own healing processes,

I discovered the healthier I became emotionally, the healthier the groups I belonged to became — an amazing discovery for me.

If this is new material for you, start by building a vocabulary for feelings; explore the relationship between your thoughts, feelings, and reactions; check to see if thoughts or feelings are subconsciously ruling your reactions when you are in a group.

Handle your stress

Be aware that emotions can be misused. Some people feel that others are there to support them emotionally by listening to their complaints and despair. Such people are emotional vampires. They come into a group and suck the life out of everyone by sharing their pain, depression, and general negativity. They may relieve some of their emotional pain, but they are also using up time and space that could be building the group's energy.

If you are one of these people, you are using your self as a weapon of destruction, not as an instrument of creativity. Learn to manage your stress and leave it at the door before you enter a group that is coming together to effect positive change. Tools to manage stress include exercise, guided imagery, relaxation methods, and a support network (coaches, family, friends, mentors).

If you have people like this in your group, you will have to establish a boundary around their negativity or the group will not perform up to expectations.

Establish boundaries — for the individual and the group

Boundaries are essential in the context of human interaction. You set a boundary to express a limitation or to control your own behavior or that of others. As humans we often set boundaries around physical, intellectual, emotional, spiritual, or sexual aspects of ourselves. As mentioned above, we may set a boundary when we believe someone is demanding too much of our emotional support or energy.

We experience our boundaries as crossed when:

- We feel discomfort because of a lack of privacy
- Our personal body space has been invaded
- Someone is in our face
- We feel crowded or claustrophobic
- Someone is touching us more than we like, even if it's friendly touching
- Touching is invasive
- We feel too much coldness and distance

Genders have different experiences of imposing boundaries around the self. Generally, due to their traditional nurturing role, women were more likely to be socialized not to impose boundaries around themselves and were encouraged to have a poor sense of their own needs, feelings, and interests so that they would be selfless and nurture the older and younger members of their family. Because of this socialization, some women have poor negotiating skills or are less able to ask that their needs be met. You may consider this an outdated view, but I regularly meet women in my workshops who have little understanding of their own personal boundaries.

In an underorganized system like a TS, an inability to express and negotiate boundaries is not helpful behavior. As soon as the initial convener puts out an idea and begins collaborating with other people, a negotiating process starts that creates the group's architecture. If individuals cannot identify their own and their organization's self-interest, articulate their needs and wants, and then enter into a never-ending process of negotiation, they will be ill-equipped to operate in a TS.

Boundaries in a TS are unclear until they are drawn, negotiated, and agreed to. Issues must be raised, and all parties must express their own boundary in order to define and negotiate what can and cannot go across it. All this is done by people in conversation and then translated into some kind of formal rule, such as terms of reference, strategic plans, policies and procedures, or informal norms that the group agrees to adopt.

Setting boundaries is not only vital to facilitate collaboration across organizations, but is also necessary to determine what the scope of the problem is and what parts of the problem can be addressed by the TS. A good vision-setting process will focus a group's vision and goals on the doable, not the impossible. In other words, a boundary (limit) must be placed on the choice of solutions. In membership policies, boundaries are set around who are members and who are prospective members. Decision-making processes need to include a time limit, a boundary that sets how long members will spend on decision making.

Once a boundary is drawn around a TS and the problem, it acts as a kind of semi-permeable membrane, protecting the organization from much of the uncertainty in the external environment. It allows TS members to reject issues or concerns that are outside the scope of the problem the TS is choosing to act upon. This means the membership is able to focus on the TS's agenda and not get sidetracked. Members can coordinate and control what goes on inside the boundary without responding to every little fluctuation outside. Without such a boundary, activities inside the organization would be wholly unpredictable and unorganized — in other words, there would be no organization.

Develop negotiation skills

Negotiation skills are crucial to TS participants. The entire development of a TS is a negotiation process. This requires that TS participants know themselves and their organization's needs and wants. They must be able to put those needs and wants on the table while others do the same. This leads to a dialogue in which they can identify options and explore how various options might satisfy some needs and interests of those around the table. Sometimes it is more productive to negotiate the criteria to assess options. All through the negotiating process, participants need to state up front what they will or won't agree to.

Develop communications skills

You can only control your side of the equation in a communication process. Therefore, in any communication you can use yourself as an instrument. The better your communication skills, the better the communication will be in any process you participate in.

The way you communicate is important. Starting a sentence with "You" signals an accusation, often accompanying blame, and it puts people on the defensive. Send "I" messages instead of starting a sentence with "You."

As a group grows, there is a direct correlation between the number of members and the amount of airtime an individual is entitled to. Everyone should have an equal share. If you are taking up more than your share of the airtime, help others claim their share. Pose direct questions to bring them into the group. If they are listening hard and thinking about the thoughts and insights other have shared, they may need to be invited into the conversation. The larger the group, the more you should be listening. This frees up space so others can use their share.

Listening is not a passive process. It is active and participatory. You must consciously give space to others. Listening to others gives you clues about their feelings, thoughts, needs, and boundaries. The contributions of group members are also pieces of data that feed into the ongoing negotiations taking place in the group. Lateral leaders foster negotiation rather than trying to impose their needs and wants on other group members.

You may have data that others don't have, and it may lead you to favor a particular course of action. Share your knowledge and the train of thought that brought you to certain conclusions so people can understand why you advocate for what you do. It is the "why" that helps people buy into certain actions or not. If everyone has the same knowledge and is aware of other members' assumptions, it allows a group to think in sync and become creative and innovative.

Become a storyteller

Often a TS, just by functioning, is developing a new story for a group or community. Proactive problem solving gives birth to a new myth and changes the way a group thinks of itself. By modeling collaboration, creating a broad-based plan, staying with conflict even if it is unresolved, and proposing to deal with problems that have been denied, you can change the story of passivity and helplessness that so many unhealthy systems and communities have assumed.

Accept conflict and learn how to resolve it

Conflict or disagreement is normal, inevitable, and resolvable. Conflict can arise when an individual or organization is not getting needs met, when there is a misunderstanding, or when assumptions are made that do not come to the surface. If you fear conflict, avoid a TS. A TS welcomes conflict because it is the way to new solutions. A TS must bring to the surface any conflict inherent in the problem set or circulating among the people responding to the problem set.

The key to conflict resolution is how you deal with conflict. You can normalize conflict situations by developing your communication skills (i.e., by using "I" statements), surfacing your assumptions, and asking clarifying questions. With these tools you will probably avoid many conflict situations that are rooted in misunderstandings.

However, in a TS the potential for conflict rises exponentially with every additional partner in the process. The task of managing all the relationships is difficult, especially if face-to-face contact is minimal. If the original members are empowered to state their needs at the beginning of the process, it establishes a norm that accepts the validity of stating need and empowers all group members to meet each other's needs and negotiate win-win solutions. Establish ground rules at the beginning of the process to set out how to fight fair and apply the win-win model for negotiating compromise.

On an individual level, the more comfortable you are with conflict, and the less your buttons get pushed (because you have disarmed them), the more others will stay calm and emulate your relaxed approach.

When you resolve conflict, you free the energy that is used to deal with hurt feelings and misunderstood communication so that it can be applied to the task and the focus of the group's work.

Learn how to influence and persuade

In a TS, we have influence but rarely any authority. As a leader in a trans-organizational system, you need to influence and encourage change in the behaviors and commitment of others on a regular basis. Most, if not all, of these people do not report to you, and you do not have the power to control them. Building and operating an effective cross-organizational team requires that you *influence* (rather than control) a wide range of organizational players, including those in the TS, those in other functions in the organizations of origin, those with higher and lower levels of authority, those from other cultures (organizational as well as social), and those who can be reticent when asked to contribute and commit.

Virtually all interactions involve an exchange. Whether the goods exchanged are overt, as in a customer-supplier relationship, or more implicit, like kindness or goodwill in a friendship, each party tends to behave with an expectation of reciprocity — an expectation that they will receive something of value from the transaction. Most of the time the concept of reciprocity is implicitly understood, and successful exchanges take place. Benevolent behavior does exist, but so do unconscious desires for equity. The concept of exchange is formalized in our culture by the market economy.

As a result, you will not successfully influence others by browbeating or cajoling them, but through an exchange of some sort. This might involve joining with others and giving and receiving cooperation. Achieving influence requires that you not only understand your own goals and frustrations, but also look at how you can understand and satisfy the needs of others. This allows you to pursue win-win outcomes that bring benefits to both parties in an exchange.

Effective influence begins with the way you view those you want to influence. If you can see each person — no matter how difficult or different he or she seems to be — as a potential ally or partner, you are halfway there. Though you may seem to be calculatedly patient, in reality you simply recognize that everyone has a legitimate stake and that you have some areas of mutual interest on which to build. Exchanging information on your needs and interests, and seeking mutual areas of benefit, are critical to the lateral leadership function of a TS.

Use tools

As much as you can, avoid becoming the advocate for a particular point of view. Instead, use tools that will increase the learning process of the whole group. Each of us in a TS holds a piece of the problem-set puzzle. Many great minds in disciplines such as sociology, social psychology, psychology, and political science have been working to develop tools and processes that enhance group learning and decision making and improve the effectiveness of groups. It's well worth finding out about these tools and using them. Check out the websites and catalogues of publishers who produce books on organization development and activism. (New Society Publishers, who published this book, are committed to that kind of material.)

The Psychology of TSs

People often behave differently in a TS than they do in their regular work environment. In a new group with unknown participants, most people will feel events are unpredictable, which can cause some to feel unsafe and experience anxiety.

Others might feel competitive and want to influence the course of events.

Until a democratic structure is in place, the TS is considered unsafe space. If there are large numbers of members, there is great potential for high anxiety. To establish safety, a group needs boundaries and continuity. We need to know who is in the group and who is not, and to have some sense that the people we connect to and trust will not suddenly vanish. Anxiety-provoking issues include:

+ Dealing with diversity
+ Dealing with differences in power and influence
+ Rivalry
+ Possible tensions between the organizations of origin and the collaboration
+ Fear of losing one's identity while creating a common identity
+ The lack of road maps
+ Unclear authority relations
+ Dealing with complexity
+ The lack of structure[3]

Although I am generally a systems thinker and pragmatist, I am also impressed by what a psychodynamic lens can bring to understanding the group life of a TS. This lens looks at the emotional level of group life — both what is conscious and what is unconscious. At the unconscious level we can explore the irrational dynamics that occur in large groups like TSs.

When a group has more than nine members, a view through this lens shows that certain unconscious forces become significant. People feel the need to make "Nobel Prize quality" contributions, which can inhibit them because they fear that their words will seem silly or inadequate. As a result, the flow of offerings that is the stuff of good conversation dries up and there is a sense of "stuckness" and lack of cohesion in the group. Productive change becomes impossible, and the status quo is reinforced by default. There is also a greater chance that unconscious processes such as projection (which involves attributing one's own thoughts, motivations, desires, feelings, and so on to someone else — having a group scapegoat is an example of this), defense mechanisms (such as repression and denial of feelings), introjecting (which means thoughtlessly assuming the behavior expected by others), and major polarization (the group degenerates into two main factions) will occur.

In lieu of traditional authority and structure, you may find the psychodynamic concept of a "container" useful. The idea is that a consultant or leader becomes a "container" and temporarily accepts the projected anxieties of group members so they can work with their fears. You may end up as a container whether you choose to or not, which is why your personal development is so important to ensuring the success of the TS. If group members are projecting their anxieties onto you, you will find it easier to sort through them if you are in tune with your own anxiety and emotional life. Identifying and sharing your emotions helps create a safe space (a container) where others can willingly share their feelings. Allowing and accepting others' emotions is the first step in creating the container. Creating the space for the group to work on the issues that emerge is the second step.

It takes time to develop sensitivity to subtle group dynamics, especially when you are involved in chairing, facilitating, or recording minutes. See if you can tune into your emotional state occasionally during meetings. Another idea is to keep a learning journal on the topic of personal development. Debrief with yourself after meetings by noting your personal feelings and recording your observation of what others were expressing as their feelings.

Lateral Leadership and Empowerment

Lateral leadership is about making space for others to assume their power and voice. You can do that by taking the following steps:

- Affirm the ability of those members who may be at risk of marginalization.
- Provide those members with opportunities to participate in the work and assume a challenge.
- Emphasize that knowledge comes through on-the-job learning and that competence increases by doing and trying.
- Affirm a sense of belonging.
- Value multiple perspectives.
- Evoke diverse role models for the entire group.
- Provide constructive feedback through questions rather than judgments.

CHAPTER 10

A Case Study

*Never doubt that a small group of thoughtful committed citizens
can change the world.*

Margaret Mead, anthropologist

In 1991, I was elected to city council for the City of York, a municipality of 140,000 people in Metro Toronto. I was elected on a platform of good governance with an agenda of progressive ideas. Unfortunately, there was little money to translate my good intentions and ideals into solid programs. Collaboration with community partners became the desirable option to achieve many of my political objectives. During my two terms as a city councilor, I was involved with the creation and development of a wonderful TS. The story of this TS, the Community Economic Development Advisory Committee (CEDAC), lets you see how TSs begin and evolve, succeed and fail. I wish I knew then what I know now!

CEDAC and the City of York

In the early 1990s the City of York was struggling with many of the same problems experienced by other former industrial communities. Job losses, government downsizing, a long-lasting recession, and a jobless recovery made local employment opportunities scarce. The nature of the economy had changed, with small businesses now creating most new jobs.

York also had some unique problems. For example, it had attracted many new immigrants because of its affordable housing and proximity to service jobs in nearby Toronto. Between 1986 and 1991, York was one of the fastest-growing municipalities in Metro Toronto, with a population growth rate of nearly four percent — almost all due to immigration. By 1991, more than half of York's residents were born outside Canada, and over 60 different language groups were represented in York. No other municipality in Canada, proportionately, had as many immigrants. This large immigrant population, with its cultural and language diversity, presented unique opportunities and challenges for a small city like York.

The educational level of York residents further complicated the situation. According to a 1994 report from the local Social Planning Council, educational levels were lower in York than anywhere else in the Greater Toronto Area (GTA). Fewer York residents had graduated from high school, trade school, or university. York students also had lower reading and writing skills than other students in the GTA.

In short, York did not have a highly skilled and educated labor force. This was part of the reason for the city's unemployment rate of 12.8 percent — three percentage points higher than that in other GTA cities. York clearly had to do something to take charge of its economic future.

From the outset, we realized that traditional economic development approaches, such as appealing to factories to relocate and mailing "lure brochures," would not address the profound economic changes taking place. The business community suggested bonuses or tax abatements in order to compete with American municipal initiatives. These types of programs were prohibited by law in Ontario, so were unavailable to us even if we had considered them to be advantageous. The CEDAC process began as a response to the devastation that was occurring in the local economy of York and Metro Toronto and in recognition of the need to try something new.

The Development Stages of a TS

Phase 1: Problem set identification

In early 1992, the mayor initiated a review of council's economic development strategy. A consultant was hired to facilitate a roundtable with 30 key stakeholders in the local economy. The consultant's report recommended that York develop a targeted labor strategy (i.e., determine the kinds of skills training our educational institutions should provide to our population), strengthen and upgrade the city's infrastructure, increase awareness of the city outside its boundaries, identify target sector opportunities (i.e., decide on certain manufacturing or commercial opportunities our city could specialize in), support the commercial retail and service sector, deliver city services more efficiently, and create a more effective approval process for new building development.

Council received these expert recommendations, but had few resources with which to attempt implementing them. York's economic development department consisted of one-and-a-half full-time staff. The department's budget was inadequate by any standard, and we could not afford outside help. In addition, council lacked models and mechanisms for making the suggested interventions in the local economy. All we had was the political will to deal with the problems facing us as a community.

The situation was not hopeless. Although York was one of Metro Toronto's smallest municipalities and was under-resourced because of its deindustrialized tax base, many millions of dollars entered our community through government programs. These funds paid for staff of social agencies, training programs, colleges, business support programs, and individual transfer payments in the form of unemployment insurance (now known as Employment Insurance) and welfare payments. We had a few community-minded corporations, individual community activists, long-established ratepayers associations, and a relatively new social planning council that was becoming skilled at reaching the multicultural communities in York.

The problem was how to mobilize all the existing resources to meet the identified challenges.

Phase 2: Motivation to collaborate

Instead of putting the consultant's report on the shelf (a course of action taken by hundreds of other communities in the same boat), council agreed with me when I said that we had to mobilize all the players in our local economy. We started the journey by establishing a small steering committee to assemble information on what other communities had done. Mayor Fergy Brown and I agreed to co-chair the process, and we had our manager of economic development, Bill Steiss, and the planning commissioner, Ed Sajecki, onside. We visited Windsor and Detroit, both cities that had established community strategic planning processes. We built a team of council and staff (some of us political adversaries) with the courage and strength to reach out to the people in our community.

This was a big step. Looking back, I realize it was unheard of in government circles at the time.

Phase 3: Member identification and selection

What an interesting phase this was. In the most politicized of all environments, we had to choose a process to determine who should be part of the community economic development process. In our small steering committee, we undertook a community mapping exercise and identified the major stakeholders in our local economy including the other three levels of government (federal, provincial, and regional), large and small businesses, business associations and business improvement areas (i.e., an association of retailers on the same street or in the same business district), the school board, ratepayers groups, the social planning council, social agencies, and self-help groups.

After identifying the stakeholder organizations, we decided that if they were headed by individuals unacceptable to members of the steering committee, we would either invite another individual from that organization or drop the organization altogether. This is not the inclusive member selection process I advocate throughout the book, but I have included the detail to show that in order to move the process forward, political decisions are often made. This political decision had ramifications down the road, as the people not invited into the process criticized CEDAC.

This phase, including the selection negotiations and organization of the first meeting, took a few months. For the first large group meeting we invited approximately 40 individuals from their respective organizations.

Phase 4: Collaborative planning

In March 1993 we held the first meeting of the TS. We told the group that it had been given a mandate by council to develop a five-year economic renewal plan for the city.

During the first few meetings we agreed on the mission statement and terms of reference for the committee. I remember trying to figure out what to do next. The group decided we needed to study the problem, so we split into three task forces, which looked at customer-focused government, human resources, and the business sector. The task forces were to assemble data on our local economy.

The collection of information proved difficult because the data compiled by numerous government bodies focused on different geographic areas. We obtained what we could and invited representatives from other government departments to make presentations to the task forces.

After three months we had received reports from both private and public sector organizations, had undertaken focus groups with the development community and small business sectors, and had come a long way toward making CEDAC a new force in York's economy.

However, the name of the committee was worrisome. A few of us felt that attaching "community" to the words "economic development" might cost us some credibility with business leaders. Community Economic Development (CED) initiatives most often emerge from the social service sector and are seen by the business community as focusing not on business creation, but on charitable projects. There was a concern that local businesses would not consider our process supportive. However, CEDAC members liked having "community" in the name, so it stuck.

Working with a large, fluid group like CEDAC presented some challenges, such as how to get everyone on the same page, make decisions, and move forward as a system. After Bill Steiss saw a presentation on facilitation processes, we decided we needed to hire a neutral facilitator to take us through a strategic planning phase. Our facilitator, from the Institute of Cultural Affairs (ICA), designed a process that included an overview of CEDAC's present situation and a discussion of members' values. Every three weeks we held a CEDAC meeting to participate in an ICA-designed group exercise. At least 25 members attended each meeting, and drop-ins were frequent.

The benefit of the ICA process was that it built consensus and understanding between disparate groups of people. The first session focused on an analysis of the current situation in York. The second session concentrated on a strategic visioning process — "what the community wanted the city to look like in five to ten years." The vision was based on four broad strategic priorities that included building a thriving, community-based "City of Distinction"; developing a vibrant city centre; creating economic support services; and facilitating vital commercial sectors.

In the next session we identified the obstacles to reaching a shared vision. These included the lack of focus to give direction to diverse sectors of the economy, inadequate processes for community participation in decision making, the lack of a business sector strategy, and the high costs of doing business.

In the fourth session we developed broad strategic directions, including how to attract, support, and retain local business; how to use our resources more effectively; and how to create more effective, future-oriented government/community partnerships.

The fifth and final session involved the community consultation phase. As one of CEDAC's assignments, several committee members trained in facilitation developed a community outreach program and facilitated meetings with seniors, ratepayers, youth, educators, multicultural groups, women, the arts community, businesses, and city staff. This work finally culminated in a Community Action Planning Day. All sector consultation participants were asked to participate.

Throughout the five sessions facilitated by the ICA consultant, the process remained open to new participants, and the facilitator incorporated newly identified issues to encourage buy-in and full participation by the community.

Immediately, smaller partnerships began forming between organizations that had never met before. The networking that happened at CEDAC meetings was one of the most important benefits of the process. We were forming social capital in our community. We watched large training organizations connect with equity groups to make the delivery of government programs in our community more accessible. Small entrepreneurs did business with, and got advice from, skilled employees of multinational organizations. It was an empowering process for everyone, including me. With the help of volunteers, institutions, and businesses, we all learned how to make things happen, and we could call upon key contacts in various community sectors.

Phase 5: Building an organization

After the strategic planning process was completed, CEDAC broke up into six task forces. One task force facilitated the community consultation phase. Another, the Subway Lobby Task Force, created and implemented a strategy to gain the support of Metro Council (the regional government, of which York was one of six members) for the Eglinton West Subway Line. In no time we had won approval for the line. Our partnership process was the envy of those communities whose transit line proposals were unsuccessful. Alas, York's success was undermined when a new provincial government was elected in June 1995 and promptly cancelled the subway line.

Under the direction of CEDAC's Strategic Niche Task Group, several studies funded by the municipal and provincial governments identified clusters of companies engaged in similar sectoral business activity. After we saw there were a number of businesses in York focused on food production and distribution, we partnered with the City of Toronto, Human Resources Development Canada, and local training providers to establish food businesses and develop a specialty food processing entrepreneurial training program.

CEDAC acted as a catalyst to spark several community-driven events. The multicultural component of CEDAC's vision morphed into the Eglinton Junior Carnival Parade, which has run every summer since 1996 and attracts more than 30,000 people every year.

CEDAC's Marketing and Image Task Group organized an open house for real estate brokers to promote the city's advantages. The city and CEDAC hired consultants to design a new logo as one of the strategies to improve the city's image. The local cable company, also a partner on CEDAC's Marketing and Image Task Group, produced a video at no charge to help market the city. Many other projects date their beginning to this initial vision.

The reality of community development is that scarce financial resources for coordination and administrative support potentially restrict what can be accomplished. The CEDAC process in the City of York was no different. Major time and energy commitments were needed to coordinate meetings, administer task forces, prepare agendas, and communicate with over 50 members. These were the days before widespread e-mail systems, but we did have fax communication. The nonprofit sector knows well that volunteer coordination should be a paid function and that money must be set aside for this purpose. A paid and dedicated staff is crucial for this process since it can be counted on to ensure the project's continuity.

City employees and I personally oversaw the ongoing implementation of the vision. We were able to hire co-op students to run committees, but we all were working flat out to keep the process moving forward. Each task group began to implement different projects, and new people were always coming into the process. Burnout loomed for me, for city staffers, and even for co-op students on four-month placements. We looked for the means to make the process sustainable.

One major grant fell through when the new provincial government was elected in 1995. The new government was ideologically opposed to supporting communities in need, so we had no hope of receiving support from it. However, the federal human resources department sat at the CEDAC table, and an innovative program consultant tried to fund the process under a labor adjustment program. First we received some end-of-year project funding. The program was not designed to fund a project like ours, so the consultant sought to expand the envelope. Soon it became obvious to many of us that we needed to develop a community economic development corporation in order to access money that would sustain the process over the long term.

CEDAC morphed into York Industrial Adjustment Services Committee (YIASC), a small committee structured and named to conform to the needs of the federal government's labor adjustment program. A paid chairperson was hired to lead the process, and decision making became centralized in this committee. Large meetings and my central coordinating/convening role disappeared. Bureaucracy reappeared. The needs of the funder became paramount. Task forces continued to meet, supported by co-op students, while the job of providing direction was slowly centralized into the YIASC committee. The focus became building a new non-profit institution, and the desire to involve many stakeholder organizations was lost. The committee did consult with stakeholders to determine the purpose of the new organization, but eventually the TS that had existed disappeared. A community economic development corporation was born from its ashes, but its energy was much different from the energy inherent in the CEDAC process. To make the story worse, the board of the new CED corporation hired a coordinator who defrauded the corporation and ended up serving a two-year sentence under house arrest.

The social capital developed in the community remained for some time, but the amalgamation of the City of York into the City of Toronto destroyed much of the community infrastructure.

I have since heard that when a multistakeholder process gets funding, the fights start. I certainly feel that the CEDAC process dissolved when it had to meet the needs of bureaucracy and evolve into something that a funder felt comfortable with, but I would rather reframe the issue to explore how these processes can be structured to maximize comfort for funders while maintaining multi-organizational commitment and flexibility.

Since the CEDAC process ended, I have experimented with this organizational building phase. Open Systems theory helped me understand the design principles, and in my consulting work with established TSs, I began customizing organizational governance systems with the flexibility needed for TSs. The evolution of information technology has helped me create effective communication and work systems with large groups. I did not get it right with CEDAC, but I am coming closer with every new TS I engage with.

Phase 6: Evaluation

To be honest, we did not even think about evaluation. Getting to the next step and the next meeting was about as far ahead as I looked at the time.

I was operating by the seat of my pants, using the force of my personality and the power that came from holding elected office. I worked with dedicated city staff and community volunteers, and through serendipity we came across tools and processes that helped us along the way. At the time I knew nothing about the different design principles or organizational power relations of trans-organizational systems. I was just beginning to understand that my personal emotional awareness and relationship-building skills were pivotal to the success of the process. I had no development framework, but did learn from some earlier models of community revitalization. Many smaller and rural communities across Canada had undertaken similar community economic strategic planning initiatives under the federal Community Futures program.

In 1996 I published an account of CEDAC in a Caledon Institute of Social Policy publication. At the time I wrote:

> CEDAC's real achievement is that it was able to show that CED [community economic development] strategic planning processes can be successful in large urban communities. We believe that people in big cities care about their communities and that they simply are not given the tools to initiate CED projects. Our tools and resources were few as well, but a coincidental convergence of staff and councillors with community development skills, combined with a long history of "rough and tumble" community politics, formed enough social capital with which to begin.

Personally, the experience and lessons learned motivate me in my work and are the raison d'être for this book. The Caledon Institute article included a section on lessons learned, but I have since realized that the goals established in our vision setting were not established with measures in mind. If we had thought about evaluation, we could have measured the accomplishments. Instead we took a community development approach and accepted credit for where we ended up, not where we wanted to go.

As more TSs are established and survive, and with management science's emphasis on providing evidence of success, effective evaluation becomes a critical part of the development process. However, evaluation must be undertaken within a conceptual framework of development, and up to now that has usually been experimental and undertaken on a one-off basis. I hope that the conceptual framework in this book can begin to provide the tools to allow for effective evaluation of TS processes outcomes.

CHAPTER 11

Conclusion

The wicked leader is he who the people despise. The good leader is he who the people revere. The great leader is he whose people say,
"We did it ourselves."

Lao Tzu

For the past three years I have presented workshops on multistakeholder processes, covering much of the material contained in this book. My students appreciate the opportunity to delve into the *how* of creating this new form of organization. Coming from the non-profit sector, many were struggling with a mandate or a job description to create multi-organizational processes without a model to follow or the resources to spend on ensuring a successful outcome. Certain questions seem to come up over and over again, including the following:

Should every new program or project be done in partnership and involve many different organizations?

I have worked for organizations with mission statements that say everything they do is done in partnership with others. This kind of approach makes for a lot of unfocused energy, and the organization often loses the chance to do what it is good at, its specialization. Creating a TS structure is a time- and energy-intensive process and should not be undertaken for every project. The assessment tools for Phases 1, 2, and 6, outlined in Chapter 3, provide a useful process to determine whether a TS is likely to succeed.

When do you bring up the question of the end of the TS? When do we disband a TS?

The best time to talk about the end is at the convention phase (Phase 4) and in the process of determining the collective vision. If you have attached time frames to your vision's strategic plan and have identified an end point, that may be a logical time to wind down the TS. You can also wrap things up with an evaluation and give participants a chance to decide whether further collaboration is desirable and, if so, what form it may take.

Of course, dysfunctional TSs are at risk of disbandment every minute of their existence. In such a situation, you may be doing everyone a favor by broaching the topic. Cessation is always an option.

What are the ultimate criteria to determine whether an organization is a TS?

A TS is accountable to its organizations of origin. Usually decisions regarding the commitment of funds or staff resources must involve the originating organizations' leadership.

Is there a name given to the magic that happens in TSs?

Management science has given the name "synergy" to the magic that happens when members of a TS are fully aligned, all systems are in place, and the strategic plan is executed. Academics in the field of management science are trying to deconstruct that magic and quantify it, as good academics are trained to do.

Are TSs a major force for societal change?

Yes, I believe so. Because of the shared power dynamics in TSs, they are more likely to evolve as DP2 organizations (see Chapter 3 for a definition and description of this type of organization). As hierarchical organizations are the breeding ground for internalized and externalized oppression in people, any democratic form of organization will result in healthier, happier people. Those people will be a major force for social change.

Do I really have to work on my personal issues to be a better TS coordinator?

Yes, the TS itself is a product of our collective imagination. It is visioned and negotiated into being. We must allow ourselves to be risk takers and visionaries and be able to let go of process and proscribed outcomes. Most of us are the products of socialization and schooling that did not encourage us to develop these abilities. Examining our emotional heritage and healing our selves is critical if we are not to replicate the same risk-averse dynamics in our groups.

Next Steps

This is often what I put as the last item on a meeting agenda — for two reasons. First, I let participants know that they develop and agree to the process plan, and second, most of the time the next steps are dependent on what was accomplished in the meeting. I would be second-guessing the activity in the meeting to know where the process will go next.

As I wrote this book and received feedback from workshop participants, new areas to explore unexpectedly emerged, including the following:

+ Creating an organizational culture for a TS
+ A good process to close down a TS

+ The potential for cybermeetings
+ Are the group dynamics in a democratic TS the same as they are in hierarchical organizations?
+ Lots more on large group dynamics
+ Good research on TS success rates in the non-profit sector

I'd love to explore all these topics, and some of them, or others, may interest you as well. You and I are organizational pioneers, and as on any frontier, we must be bold and go forth to explore.

Summary

We started this journey learning about trans-organizational systems by looking at the concept of organization itself. Although usually invisible to us, organizations are, in fact, one of the most important characteristics of modern society. Our global economic systems are based on the modern organizational form that we have turned into multinational corporations and nation-state government. By developing the organization, we produced a mechanism that could achieve goals beyond the reach of the individual, transcending earlier communal forms of association based on individual relations with relatives, friends, and acquaintances, to create associative forms based on contractual arrangements.

Throughout this book I have argued that in the later part of the 20th century, the nature and complexity of problems led us to a new form of organization — the TS. TSs are an organizational response to our turbulent times. They are a tool and a strategy to deal with complexity. Those who work in human services or private business — anyone who wishes to tackle the challenging problems of our time — quickly comes to the understanding that they need to take a systems view of the problem or problem set they are trying to solve.

Academics can devote their lives to gaining an understanding of the problem and its systemic roots. Academic analyses fill our libraries. However, few of those well-thought-out solutions result in systemic change, mainly because translating desirable solutions into action requires the participation of the players who belong to the system in question. If a convener understands this and attempts to have system players participate, it creates an opportunity for systemic change. When those system players are involved in collective analysis and decision making, the result is a trans-organizational system.

In North America, we have been moving away from the metaphors and assumptions of the industrial economy. We no longer think of men and women or organizations as machines. Rather, we are embracing a holistic perspective and acknowledging that we are emotional beings as well as rational, thinking persons.

We see over and over that change cannot happen when the participants in a human system resist with all of their hearts and minds.

At the same time, people are becoming more educated to meet the demands of the knowledge economy. Their creativity is critical if organizations are to overcome the challenges of adapting to the complexity of the global economy, and that creativity cannot be bought or extracted forcefully from people who are oppressed, either internally or externally. It is not in the interests of the knowledge economy to control people by force and fear.

Related to this is the need for more people to take leadership roles. As most of our assumptions about leadership are associated with hierarchical forms of organization, it is not easy to think of leadership as something associated with rank-and-file members. From the time I was a child, I have been interested in leadership and have been pegged as a "leader." But I avoided seeking positions of responsibility. It was not until after I became a mother and felt I was in the most important leadership role of my life that I started to think about what the term could mean. The concept of feminine leadership emerged in the 1980s and resonated with me. This was when the feminine-identified leadership skill of nurturing was transformed into the more gender-neutral concept of "coaching." Competencies in skills such as persuading and influencing became important tools for success, while the managerial model of control and command fell out of favor. What I think is new is the evolving model of leadership exercised by all, not just one or a few in a system. Different elements of leadership are necessary at different times in the life of a TS, and all participants must step up with their particular leadership ability and skill set when the opportunity presents itself for their contribution. This form of leadership is the most renewable and sustainable, providing a never-ending supply of leaders.

We are growing new types of people who need democratic and soul-nurturing workplaces to support their creative power, explore new opportunities, and solve the world's problems. In certain situations a trans-organizational system can be that new kind of workplace and encourage its members to think and act out of the box, share their collective knowledge and resources, and make incredible change happen.

Endnotes

Chapter 1

1. Canadian Labour Congress. *Is Work Working for You?* [online]. [Cited October 13, 2003]. Report prepared for the Canadian Labour Congress for Labour Day 2001. <www.working4you.ca/report2002.html>

2. Paul Rutherford. *Endless Propaganda: The Advertising of Public Goods.* University of Toronto Press, 2000.

3. Lee Hanson. "Society and self-managing teams." *International Journal of Social Economics.* Vol. 25, no. 1 (1998), p. 82.

4. Rutherford. *Endless Propaganda.* p. 115.

5. Bruce Alexander. "Getting at the roots of addiction." *The Globe & Mail.* July 20, 2001.

6. Stefan Kipfer and Roger Keil. *Still Planning to Be Different? Toronto at the Turn of the Millennium* [online]. [Cited September 23, 2002]. Faculty of Environmental Studies, York University, 2000. <www.yorku.ca/rkeil/kipferkeil.htm>

7. Thomas Homer-Dixon. *The Ingenuity Gap: How Can We Solve the Problems of the Future?* Knopf, 2000.

8. Don Tapscott, Alex Lowy, and David Ticholl. *Blueprint for the Digital Economy.* McGraw Hill, 1998, p. 266.

9. Don De Guerre and Merrilyn Emery. *Introduction to Open Systems: Learning and Doing What Work.* Centre for Human Relations and Community Studies, Concordia University, 2000.

10. Quoted in Merrilyn Emery and Ron Purser. *The Search Conference: A Powerful Method for Planning Organizational Change and Community Action.* Jossey Bass, 1996, pp. 54, 277.

11. Eric Trist originated the term "organizational ecology," which is discussed in Merrilyn Emery and Ron Purser. *The Search Conference,* p. 278.

12. Robert Kanigel. *The One Best Way: Frederick Winslow Taylor and the Enigma of Efficiency*. Viking Press, 1997.

13. Penelope Hawe and Alan Shiell. "Social Capital and Health Promotion: A Review" [online]. [Cited June 22, 2002]. Department of Public Health and Community Medicine, University of Sydney, n.d. <www.health.nsw.gov.au/public-health/health-promotion/hpss/capacity building/indexcbintro.htm>

14. Leslie F. Seidle. *Social Partnerships: Fostering Citizen Participation and Public Sector Responsiveness*. Unpublished paper presented at IPAC Conference ("Making Connections, Building Relationships: An Agenda for Action"), Toronto, 1995.

Chapter 2

1. Peter F. Drucker. *Post-Capitalist Society*. HarperCollins, 1993, p. 46.

2. Drucker. *Post-Capitalist Society*, p. 50.

3. Thomas G. Cummings and Christopher G. Worley. *Organization Development and Change*. Southwestern College Publishing, 1996, p. 467.

4. List devised by Yoshino and Rangan and cited in David Knoke and Emanuela Todeva. *Strategic Alliances and Corporate Social Capital* [online]. [Cited October 4, 2002]. University of Minnesota, May 2001. <www.soc.umn.edu/~knoke/pages/Todeva&Knoke.pdf>

5. Arthur T. Himmelman. *Collaboration for a Change* [online] [cited May, 2003]. January 2002. <www.futurehealth.ucsf.edu/pdf_files/4achange.pdf>

6. William Bergquist, Juli Betwee, and David Meuel. *Building Strategic Partnerships: How to Extend Your Organization's Reach Through Partnerships, Alliances and Joint Ventures*. Jossey Bass, 1995, p. 6.

Chapter 3

1. Merrilyn Emery. *Searching: The Theory and Practice of Making Cultural Change*. John Benjamins, 1999.

2. Thomas G. Cummings. "Trans-organizational Development." *Research in Organizational Behaviour*. Vol 6 (1984), p. 390.

3. Neil Rackham, Lawrence Freidman, and Richard Ruff. *Getting Partnering Right*. McGraw Hill, 1996, p. 132.

4. Barbara Gray. *Collaborating: Finding Common Ground for Multiparty Problems*. Jossey Bass, 1989, p. 92.

5. Quoted in Merrilyn Emery, ed. *Participative Design for Participative Democracy*. Centre for Continuing Education, Australian National University, 1993, p. 173.

Chapter 4

1. Quoted in Barbara Gray. *Collaborating: Finding Common Ground for Multiparty Problems*. Jossey Bass, 1989, p. 28.

2. Leslie F. Seidle. *Social Partnerships: Fostering Citizen Participation and Public Sector Responsiveness*. Unpublished paper presented at IPAC Conference ("Making Connections, Building Relationships: An Agenda for Action"), Toronto, 1995, p. 3.

3. Ibid.

Chapter 6

1. Sarah Powell. "Guru Interview" (interview with Edgar Schein) [online]. [Cited October 13, 2002]. <www.managementfirst.com/articles/schein.htm>

2. Geerte Hofstede. *Culture's Consequences: International Differences in Work-related Values*. Sage, 1980.

3. Brian Wampler. *A Guide to Participatory Budgeting* [online]. [Cited October 23, 2003], p. 3. <www.internationalbudget.org/resources/library/GPB.pdf>

4. Leslie Ehle. *Mythic Transformation, An interview with Harrison Owen* [online]. [Cited September 13, 2003]. *Living Business*. IC#11 (Autumn 1985), p. 40. <www.context.org/ICLIB/IC11/Owen.htm>

Chapter 7

1. Ron Ashkenas, Dave Ulrich, Todd Jich, and Steve Kerr. *The Boundaryless Organization*. Jossey Bass, 1995, p. 185.

Chapter 8

1. Ann Svendsen. *The Stakeholder Strategy*. Berrett-Koehler, 1998, p. 147.

2. Thomas G. Cummings and Christopher G. Worley. *Organization Development and Change*. Southwestern College Publishing, 1996, p. 471.

Chapter 9

1. William Bergquist, Juli Betwee, and David Meuel. *Building Strategic Partnerships: How to Extend Your Organization's Reach Through Partnerships, Alliances and Joint Ventures*. Jossey Bass, 1995, p. 43.

2. Merrilyn Emery. *Searching: The Theory and Practice of Making Cultural Change*. John Benjamins, 1999.

3. Sylvia Prins. *Emerging Coordination Processes in Multiparty Collaboration: A Psychodynamic Perspective.* Unpublished paper presented at EIASM doctoral seminar, Brussels, May 7-11, 2001, p. 14.

Bibliography

Ackoff, R.L. and Fred Emery. *On Purposeful Systems.* Tavistock Publications, 1972.

Alban, Billie T. and Barbara Benedict Bunker. *The Change Handbook.* Jossey Bass, 1996.

Alexander, Bruce. "Getting at the Roots of Addiction." *The Globe and Mail.* July 20, 2001.

American Journal of Health Promotion. special issue "Social Ecology." Vol. 10, no. 4 (March/April 1996).

Arnstein, Sherry. "Eight Rungs on a Ladder of Citizen Participation." *Journal of the Institute of American Planners.* Vol. 35, no. 4 (1969), pp. 216-224.

Ashkenas, Ron, Dave Ulrich, Todd Jich, and Steve Kerr. *The Boundaryless Organization.* Jossey Bass, 1995.

Austin, James E. "Principles for Partnership" [online]. [Cited August 27, 2002]. *Leader to Leader.* no. 18 (Fall 2000). <www.pfdf.org/leaderbooks/l2l/fall2000/austin.html>

Austin, James E. and Frances Hesselbein. *Meeting the Collaboration Challenge: Developing Strategic Alliances Between Non-profit Organizations and Businesses.* [online]. [Cited August 15, 2002]. The Drucker Foundation and Jossey Bass. <www.drucker.org/collaboration/challenge/pdfs/mtcc complete.pdf>

Beck-Kritek, Phyllis. *Negotiating at an Uneven Table.* John Wiley and Sons, 2002.

Bergquist, William, Juli Betwee, and David Meuel. *Building Strategic Partnerships: How to Extend Your Organization's Reach Through Partnerships, Alliances and Joint Ventures.* Jossey Bass, 1995.

Block, Peter. *Flawless Consulting.* Jossey Bass/Pfeiffer, 1981.

Bradshaw, Catherine, Joan Roberts, and Sylvia Cheuy. "The Search Conference: A Participative Planning Method that Builds Widespread Collaboration" and "Real Collaboration Requires Power Sharing." In *The Collaborative Work Systems Fieldbook: Strategies for Building Successful Teams,* edited by Michael M. Beyerlein, Gerald Klein, and Laurie Broedling. John Wiley and Sons, 2003.

Broom, Michael F. and Donald C. Klein. *Power: The Infinite Game*. Sea Otter Press, 1999.

Bunker, Barbara and Billie Alban. *Large Group Interventions: Engaging the Whole System for Rapid Change*. Jossey Bass, 1997.

Cabana, Steven and Janet D. Fiero. "Motorola, Strategic Planning and the Search Conference." *Journal for Quality and Participation*. July/August 1995.

Canadian Labour Congress. *Is Work Working for You?* [online]. [Cited October 13, 2003]. Report prepared for the Canadian Labour Congress for Labour Day 2001. <www.working4you.ca/report2002.html>

Canadian Public Health Association. *The Canadian Experience of Intersectoral Collaboration for Health Gains*. 1997.

Clement, W.R. *Quantum Jump: A Survival Guide of the New Renaissance*. Insomniac Press, 1998.

Cummings, Thomas G. "Trans-organizational Development." *Research in Organizational Behaviour*, JAI Press. Vol. 6 (1984), pp 367-422.

Cummings, Thomas G. and Christopher G. Worley. *Organization Development and Change*. Southwestern College Publishing, 1996.

De Greene, Kenyon B. *A Systems-based Approach to Policymaking*. Kluwer Academic Publishers, 1993.

De Guerre, Don and Merrilyn Emery. *Introduction to Open Systems: Learning and Doing What Work*. Centre for Human Relations and Community Studies, Concordia University, 2000.

Devane, Tom and Peggy Holman. *The Change Handbook: Group Methods for Shaping the Future*. Berrett-Koehler, 1999.

Drucker, Peter F. *Post-Capitalist Society*. HarperCollins, 1993.

Ehle, Leslie. *Mythic Transformation: An Interview with Harrison Owen* [online]. [Cited on September13, 2003]. *Living Business*. no. 11 (Autumn 1985), p. 40 <www.context.org/ICLIB/IC11/Owen.htm>

Emery, Merrilyn, ed. *Participative Design for Participative Democracy*. Centre for Continuing Education, Australian National University, 1993.

Emery, Merrilyn. *Searching: The Theory and Practice of Making Cultural Change*. John Benjamins, 1999.

Emery, Merrilyn and Ron Purser. *The Search Conference: A Powerful Method for Planning Organizational Change and Community Action*. Jossey Bass, 1996.

Evans, Jeff and Liz Thach. "Towards the Next Generation Change Model." *OD Practitioner*. Vol. 32, no 4 (2000).

Fiero, Janet D. and Craig E. McGee. "Turbulent Environments Require Fast, Flat and Flexible Organizations." *OD Practitioner*. Vol. 32, no. 4 (2000).

Fisher, Roger and Alan Sharp. *Getting It Done: How to Lead When You Are Not In Charge*. HarperCollins, 1998.

Fortin, J.P., G. Groleau, V. Lemieux, M. O'Neill, and P. Lamarch. *Intersectoral Action for Health: Summary of Research Findings*. Laval University, 1994.

Frank, Flo and Anne Smith. *The Partnership Handbook*. The Caledon Institute, 1997.

Gilchrist, Alison. "The Well-connected Community: Networking to the Edge of Chaos." *Community Development Journal*. Vol. 35, no. 3 (2000), pp. 264-275.

Goleman, Daniel. *Working With Emotional Intelligence*. Bantam Books, 1998.

Gray, Barbara. *Collaborating: Finding Common Ground for Multiparty Problems*. Jossey Bass, 1989.

Gray, Barbara. "Human Relations: Conditions Facilitating Interorganizational Collaboration." *Human Relations*. Vol. 38 (1985), pp. 911-936.

Hanson, Lee. "Society and Self-managing Teams." *International Journal of Social Economics*, MCB University Press. Vol. 25, no. 1 (1998), pp. 72-89.

Hawe, Penelope and Alan Shiell. "Social Capital and Health Promotion: A Review" [online]. [Cited June 22, 2002]. Department of Public Health and Community Medicine, University of Sydney. n.d. <www.health.nsw.gov.au/ public-health/health-promotion/hpss/capacitybuilding/indexcbintro.htm>

Health Canada. *Achieving Health for All: A Framework for Health Promotion*. 1986.

Health Canada. "Toward a Healthy Future: Second Report on the Health of Canadians" [online]. [Cited May 14, 2003]. Health Canada, Population Health Approach Website. 1999. <www.hc-sc.gc.ca/hppb/phdd/determinants/determinants.html#social>

Hesselbein, Frances, Marshall Goldsmith, and Richard Beckard, eds. *The Organization of the Future*. Jossey Bass, 1997.

Himmelman, Arthur, T. *Collaboration for a Change* [online]. [cited May, 2003], January 2002. <www.futurehealth.ucsf.edu/pdf_files/4achange.pdf>.

Hofstede, Geerte. *Culture's Consequences: International Differences in Work-related Values*. Sage, 1980.

Homer-Dixon, Thomas. *The Ingenuity Gap: How Can We Solve the Problems of the Future?* Knopf, 2000.

Jacobs, Jane. *Systems of Survival.* Random House, 1994.

Kaner, Sam, Sara Fisk, and Lenny Lind. *Facilitator's Guide to Participatory Decision-Making.* New Society Publishers, 1996.

Kanigel, Robert. *The One Best Way: Frederick Winslow Taylor and the Enigma of Efficiency.* Viking Press, 1997.

Kass, R. *Theories of Small Group Development.* 2nd edition. Centre for Human Relations and Community Studies, Concordia University, 1998.

Kemmis, Daniel. *Community and the Politics of Place.* University of Oklahoma Press, 1990.

Kipfer, Stefan and Roger Keil. *Still Planning to Be Different? Toronto at the Turn of the Millennium* [online]. [Cited September 23, 2002]. Faculty of Environmental Studies, York University, 2000. <www.yorku.ca/rkeil/kipferkeil.htm>

Knoke, David and Emanuela Todeva. *Strategic Alliances and Corporate Social Capital* [online]. [Cited October 4, 2002]. University of Minnesota, May 2001. <www.soc.umn.edu/~knoke/pages/Todeva&Knoke.pdf>

Kretzmann, John P. and John L. McKnight. *Building Communities from the Inside Out: A Path Toward Finding and Mobilizing a Community's Assets.* Institute for Policy Research, 1993.

Kuhn M., C. Doucet, and N. Edwards. *Effectiveness of Coalitions in Heart Health Promotion, Tobacco Use Reduction and Injury Prevention: A Systematic Review of the Literature, 1990-1998.* University of Ottawa, 1999.

Lippet, Lawrence L. *Preferred Futuring.* Berrett-Koehler, 1998.

Manske, Stephen D. and Catherine O. Maule, eds. "A System for Best Practices." *Best Practices in Addiction.* Vol. 21, no. 6 (December 2001/Janaury 2002).

Morgan, Gareth. *Images of Organization: The Executive Edition.* Berrett-Koehler, 1998.

Murphy, Brian K. *Transforming Ourselves, Transforming our World: An Open Conspiracy for Social Change.* Fernwood Publishing, 1999.

Nelson, Gary M. *Self Governance in Communities and Families.* Berrett-Koehler, 2000.

Nye, Nancy and Norman J. Glickman. *Expanding Capacity through Local Community Development Partnerships.* Report for the Ford Foundation, Center for Urban Policy Research, Rutgers State University, 1995.

Oshry, Barry. *Seeing Systems: Unlocking the Mysteries of Organizational Life.* Berrett-Koehler, 1996.

Owen, Harrison. *Open Space Technology: A User's Guide.* Abbott Publishing, 1992.

Owen, Harrison. *Spirit: Transformation and Development in Organizations.* Abbott Publishing, 1987.

Powell, Sarah. "Guru Interview" (Interview with Edgar Schein) [online]. [Cited October 13, 2002]. <www.managementfirst.com/articles/schein.htm>

Prins, Sylvia. *Emerging Coordination Processes in Multiparty Collaboration: A Psychodynamic Perspective.* Unpublished paper presented at EIASM doctoral seminar, Brussels, May 7-11, 2001.

Rackham, Neil, Lawrence Freidman, and Richard Ruff. *Getting Partnering Right.* McGraw Hill, 1996.

Rifkin, Jeremy. *The Age of Access.* Putnam, 2000.

Roberts, Joan. "The Community Economic Development Advisory Committee for the City of York: A Municipal Government Partnership" [online]. [Cited September 26, 2002]. *Perspectives on Partnerships: The Social Partnerships Project.* Caledon Institute of Social Policy, June 1998. <www.caledoninst.org/perspect.pdf>

Roulier, Monte. "Searching for Healthy Communities: Can Search Conferences Help our Communities get Healthy and Stay that Way?" *National Civic Review.* Vol. 86, no 1 (1997).

Rutherford, Paul. *Endless Propaganda: The Advertising of Public Goods.* University of Toronto Press, 2000.

Schein, Edgar. *Process Consultation: Its Role in Organization Development.* Addison-Wesley Publishing, 1969.

Schwartz, Roger. *The Skilled Facilitator.* Jossey Bass, 1994.

Seel, Richard. "Anxiety and Incompetence in the Large Group: A Psychodynamic Perspective." *Journal of Organizational Change Management.* Vol. 14, no 5 (2001), pp. 493-504.

Seidle, Leslie F. *Social Partnerships: Fostering Citizen Participation and Public Sector Responsiveness.* Unpublished paper presented at IPAC Conference ("Making Connections, Building Relationships: An Agenda for Action"), Toronto, 1995.

Senge, Peter. *The Fifth Discipline.* Doubleday, 1994.

Senge, Peter, Art Kleiner, Charlotte Roberts, Richard Ross, and Bryan Smith. *The Fifth Discipline Fieldbook: Strategies and Tools for Building A Learning Organization.* Doubleday/Currency, 1994.

Senge, Peter, Art Kleiner, Charlotte Roberts, Richard Ross, and Bryan Smith. *The Dance of Change: The Challenges of Sustaining Momentum in Learning Organizations.*

Doubleday/Currency, 1999.

Spencer, Laura. *Winning Through Participation.* Kendall/Hunt Publishing Company, 1989.

Starhawk. *Truth or Dare: Encounters with Power, Authority, and Mystery.* HarperCollins Canada. 1990.

Svendsen, Ann. *The Stakeholder Strategy.* Berrett-Koehler, 1998.

Tapscott, Don, Alex Lowy, and David Ticholl. *Blueprint for the Digital Economy.* McGraw Hill, 1998.

Tapscott, Don, Alex Lowy, and David Ticholl. *Digital Capital: Harnessing the Power of Business Webs.* Harvard Business School Press, 2000.

Trist, Eric. *The Evolution of Socio-technical Systems.* Ontario Quality of Working Life Centre, 1981.

Tuckman, B. "Developmental Sequence in Small Groups." *Psychological Bulletin.* vol. 63 (1965), pp. 384-399.

Wampler, Brian. *A Guide to Participatory Budgeting* [online]. [Cited on October 23, 2003]. <www.internationalbudget.org/resources/library/GPB.pdf>

The Warren Company. *A.S.A.P. Alliance Workbook* [online]. [Cited on July 3, 2002]. <www.warrenco.com>

Weisbord, Marvin, R. *Discovering Common Ground.* Berrett-Koehler, 1992.

Weiss, Elisa, Rebecca Miller, and Roz Lasker. *Findings from the National Study of Partnership Functioning: Report to the Partnerships that Participate* [online]. [Cited on February 17, 2002]. The Center for the Advancement of Collaborative Strategies in Health, Division of Public Health, New York Academy of Medicine, 2001. <www.cacsh.org/pdf/StudyReport.pdf>

Wondolleck, Julia M. and Steven L. Yaffee. *Sustaining the Success of Collaborative Partnerships: Revisiting the Building Bridges Cases* [online]. [Cited on January 21, 2002]. University of Michigan, 1997. <www.snre.umich.edu/emi/collaboration/publications.htm>

Wondolleck, Julia M. and Steven L. Yaffee. *Making Collaboration Work: Lessons from Innovation in Natural Resources* [online]. [Cited on January 21, 2002]. University of Michigan, 1997. <www.snre.umich.edu/emi/collaboration/publications.html>

World Health Organization. *Intersectoral Action for Health: A Cornerstone for Health for All in the Twenty-First Century.* Report on an international conference held in Halifax, April 20-23, 1997.

Index

About the Author

JOAN ROBERTS M.A. has over 20 years of experience managing projects, developing organizations and working with different levels of government. Joan's work focuses on building collaborative processes that engage members to enhance and improve their service delivery. Her skill set includes high level knowledge and hands on experience of the fields of change management, communications and governance.

She is a former city councilor and for the last six years has run her own consulting and training practice

In the early '90s, she created a trans- 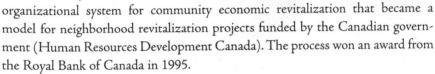 organizational system for community economic revitalization that became a model for neighborhood revitalization projects funded by the Canadian government (Human Resources Development Canada). The process won an award from the Royal Bank of Canada in 1995.

She holds a Masters Degree in Organization Development and has designed and delivered workshops on advocacy, economic development, governance, multistakeholder processes and governance.

If you have enjoyed *Alliances, Coalitions and Partnerships,*
you might also enjoy other

BOOKS TO BUILD A NEW SOCIETY

Our books provide positive solutions for people who want to
make a difference. We specialize in:

Environment and Justice ✦ Conscientious Commerce
Sustainable Living ✦ Ecological Design and Planning
Natural Building & Appropriate Technology ✦ New Forestry
Educational and Parenting Resources ✦ Nonviolence
Progressive Leadership ✦ Resistance and Community

For a full list of NSP's titles, please call **1-800-567-6772** *or check out our web site at:*

www.newsociety.com

New Society Publishers

ENVIRONMENTAL BENEFITS STATEMENT

New Society Publishers has chosen to produce this book on recycled paper made from
100% post consumer waste, processed chlorine free, and old growth free.

For every 5,000 books printed, New Society saves the following resources:[1]

31	Trees
2,777	Pounds of Solid Waste
3,056	Gallons of Water
3,986	Kilowatt Hours of Electricity
5,049	Pounds of Greenhouse Gases
22	Pounds of HAPs, VOCs, and AOX Combined
8	Cubic Yards of Landfill Space

[1]Environmental benefits are calculated based on research done by the Environmental Defense Fund and
other members of the Paper Task Force who study the environmental impacts of the paper industry.

NEW SOCIETY PUBLISHERS